Black Cat Tales:

History and Hauntings of Old Salem

Daniel and Lara Fury

For our parents,
Kristin and Thomas, Susan and Don,
who put a lot of faith in two crazy kids
and their love of ghost stories.

For Godsteve, Comet, Marco, Rameses, Meesha, Muta, Summer,
Ebi-chan, and of course Gypsy, who gave it all a name.
And for all the cats whose lives have touched ours over the years,
and will in the future.

And for everyone in our stories,
you are so much more than words on a page,
you are real, honest people, whose voices should be heard.
You are Legend.

Table Of Contents

Introduction

I t was a dark and stormy night, because all of the best nights truly are. We had just moved into our first house in Salem, a beautiful 1782 structure built for Nathaniel Chamberlain, a bricklayer who had worked on Elias Haskett Derby's Grand Turk, the first New England ship to sail to China from the colonies. Needless to say, the house had a lot of history, and though it needed quite a bit of work, we were thrilled with it and all of its mysteries and quirks.

We moved in with our three cats; the Japanese Bobtail, Muta, a little girl who loves nothing more than snuggles and more snuggles, and has been my ever present shadow during the writing of this book, our big black Maine Coon, Rameses, the poster boy for this book and our tour company, who loves to run around at all hours of the night like a fluffy cannonball, and Marco, our quiet grey Maine Coon who used to live in an antique bookstore in Maine before coming to us many years ago.

On this stormy night, Rameses had already hidden somewhere unfathomable (he's afraid of thunder), Muta was fast asleep, and Marco was making his late night patrols around the house. As was to be expected in an older house in an historic neighborhood, it was only a matter of time before we lost power. Gathering some candles and heading to the parlor, our new old house was alive with creaks and squeaks and things that went bump in the night. We began to talk about what it must have been like for each successive generation who had the good fortune to share in the history of this home. Merchants to foreign lands had once walked these same wide pine floorboards, and we were so fortunate to have found a place with such rich history.

The candlelight flickered as the storm grew more intense, and out of the corner of my eye I caught movement. At first I dismissed it as a trick of the moving light, combined with the overall eerie atmosphere of the evening and conversation. But no, as I turned my head there was certainly something there, if only for the briefest of moments.

What it was, I could not rightly say; a spectral sphere of incomprehensible substance was floating through the air, past the fireplace, past the china cabinet, past the doorway to the secret pass-through, and then, without pausing a moment, out through the wall by the window. It vanished within half the span of a breath, and I turned to my husband to tell him what I had seen, managing to get only so far as a, "Did you just see…" before our quiet grey cat Marco tore into the room like a bolt of lightning himself, following the course the inscrutable phantom had taken.

With a powerful leap he sprang forward to where it had vanished into the wall, and created a mighty thud with his front paws. He looked frustrated and confused for a few moments, then, with nary a backwards glance, returned to his evening rounds.

Clearly, we had a ghost hunting cat.

Over the past 5 years, we have taken our love of history and fascination with the supernatural, and developed our company, Black Cat Tours, into a place where the visitors of Salem can learn about the true histories that make up so many amazing stories of a city that truly has magic in its blood. We have been fortunate to hear so many fantastic tales of ghostly visits, creepy encounters, and unexplainable events that we decided it was high time to put them all together in a way that shared the eerie tales with our passionate research into the antiquity behind them. We know that not everyone can make the visit to Salem, so we hope by bringing it to you in these stories, you will feel like you are truly walking the cobblestone streets with us, and experiencing the chills that only the Witch City can bring you.

And if you have been fortunate enough to see Salem with your own eyes, think of this book as a way to take home all of the venerable tales, and maybe a ghost or two with you!

Second Introduction:
A Statement About History

Over the course of writing this book, the history grew in the telling. It began, as we stated, as a way to share our tour with those who could not travel to Salem, and was a way of putting our spoken words to paper. It became clear very early on that without the confines of a specific time frame and with the ability to "travel" to places we could not normally take our guests, that we would want to include as much information and as many locations as we could.

What fascinates us is what Cotton Mather would have referred to as "The Invisible World" and so that is how we refer to it here. Our ghost stories are the truest accounts that we can find as it relates to these locations. Some of our tales are modern descriptions of paranormal activities that occurred up to a few weeks before the publication of this book, while others are stories that go back to the Witchcraft Hysteria of 1692. The testimony of the people involved in that terrifying time are often far more horrific than most tend to think of. The men, women, and children involved in the "afflictions" were the victims of such unbelievable acts of horror that they could (and did) frighten the witnesses so badly that "spectral evidence" was all that was needed to convict innocent men and women to hang for the crimes. We do not in any way condone or agree with the statements of the "afflicted" but we feel they are worth including as paranormal phenomena, as we cannot speak with those who supposedly experienced the events.

It was just after the Civil War that the fascination with the afterlife and supernatural would begin to peak, as grieving families looked for a way to communicate with lost loved ones, and visiting Spiritualists (or Mediums) or using Spirit Boards would become a common pastime. While no definitive proof has ever been presented of the existence of life after death, it is perhaps our hope to cling to the possibility of immortality and existence in the Invisible World.

Salem today is filled with psychics and paranormal investigators, and nearly every building has some tale told in the dark of night of phenomenon that the earthly mind cannot explain. To do justice to these stories and the very real people involved in them, our tales are often more History than Haunting. We feel it is just as important and chilling (if not more so), to know why these sites are supposedly a hotbed of supernatural phenomena, than it is to simply tell you which window might yield the best ghost photo.

Therefore if you are simply looking for the hauntings without the history, we will say that this may not be the book for you, but we hope that you will be drawn in by the true stories told herein, and become as fascinated by them as we were.

The Old Burying Point Cemetery:
Blackbeard's Ghost

51 Charter Street, Salem

L ong shadows creep across lichen crusted stones that protrude from the earth like the nails of a dead man's hand, as a hawk screeches down to hunt for prey amidst the ancient tombs. Throngs of the undead stalk battered pathways that wind about the dying grass and lightning struck trees, poring over the scrawled names of the long deceased denizens of this quaint New England town. The scene would not be amiss in any terrifying horror flick of the silver screen, and unsurprisingly, a query is shouted out into the crisp autumn air, punctuated by the crunching of footsteps in the blanket of fallen leaves:

"Is that a real cemetery?"

The Old Burying Point Cemetery is the city's oldest, the first interment unknown, but likely going as far back as the mid 1630s, and yes, it is indeed a real cemetery, officially set aside for the burial of the dead in 1637. We give the tourists a pass for the question, as time and nature have aged the site far more perfectly than any Hollywood set dresser could manage. The site is, however, far more interesting than any concocted fabrication of film, and is the final resting place of some of our fair city's most illustrious figures, and the most gruesome spectre the city can conjure.

Among the stones are the grave markers for Richard More, who travelled on the Mayflower to the New World against his will as an indentured servant. Richard's father Samuel had discovered that his wife had been unfaithful and none of their four children were his. After their divorce, Samuel had booked passage for Richard and his three siblings as servants. Only Richard survived. He made the best of his situation, however, and after years of work he made his way up the social ladder to become a successful sea captain and merchant, living to the ripe old age of 81, and married twice, our first example of the fulfillment of the American Dream.

Samuel McIntire, the designer of many of our city's most beautiful homes and municipal buildings (with an entire district named for him) is buried here, along with Nathaniel Mather, brother of Cotton Mather, who played such a large role in Salem's Witchcraft Hysteria.

Perhaps the most famous permanent resident of the Old Burying Point is John Hathorne, great, great grandfather of Nathaniel Hawthorne, known to many as the "Hanging Judge" but in reality only one of nine judges of the Court of Oyer and Terminer, though perhaps the most vocal. It was he and Jonathan Corwin who were magistrates during the early days of the Hysteria, and therefore their questioning makes up a large portion of the documents that have passed down to us from the court scribes. Hathorne was an active participant in King William's War following the Trials, and was promoted to Colonel in the militia in 1711, though he had many mishaps during his time in the military.

Many people believe that Nathaniel changed his last name to distance himself from his ancestors actions (which he was very vocally opposed to) by adding the "W" in his last name. This is a pervasive rumor, but it is far more likely that it was added simply to aid pronunciation, as spelling was not standardized until the 1800s. Buried nearby in the family plot is also Nathaniel's grandfather, "Bold" Daniel Hathorne, a war hero during the Revolution, who made up for his grandfather's shortcomings as a soldier, nearly single-handedly capturing a British vessel in such a daring feat that he had a popular tavern song written for him.

The ghost of The Old Burying Point is not related to any of these legendary figures however, and his relationship to Salem is far more adversarial. In the early 1700s, the survivors of the pirate captain, Black Sam Bellamy's crew on board the Whydah and Mary Anne were transported to the Boston Jail, which raised the ire of the most infamous pirate of all time, Edward Teach, known by his menacing moniker, "Blackbeard."

In retaliation for the actions against his former compatriot, Teach put out a bounty on any ships sailing from Massachusetts, and it was during this time that legends state Teach himself visited Salem, after plundering and burning a ship from Boston. Under cover of darkness, his crew crept up the South River in small boats to hold a meeting in the back of the Old Burying Point Cemetery, which in those days was directly on the shore of the river, and part of the largest port on the Eastern Seaboard. The far side of the cemetery from Charter Street, a high embankment with a stone wall, was once a sloping beach, an easy place for scurvy knaves to hide their dark deeds from the townsfolk.

A master showman, the man known as the "King of Pirates" would do his damndest during his reign of terror to convince laymen and sailors alike that he was the Devil himself, lighting fuses in his beard during battle so that his face would be wreathed in smoke. He would spread word through his lackeys in the local taverns that people had better stay away from places like the Old Burying Point, for if they heard evil laughter and the light of lamps, it was the sounds of ghosts and ghouls, and they, being a superstitious lot, would follow the advice gratefully. No one knows for certain what transpired during Blackbeard's secret convocations, perhaps he was planning a jailbreak in nearby Boston, though some say a duel was fought here, and one of his crew was buried in a conveniently recent dug grave.

This alleged visit and desire for revenge is not the only connection Blackbeard has to the Old Burying Point, nor is it the most macabre. On November 22nd, 1718, Edward Teach's reign was finally brought to an end by the fearless Lieutenant Maynard, who chased down Blackbeard's sloop Adventure off the coast of North Carolina, with Maynard reporting that he "drank Damnation to me and my men, whom he stil'd Cowardly Puppies, saying He would neither give nor take Quarter." A fierce battle took place, and it was only after a dozen or so men surrounded Teach that he finally fell to his wounds. Maynard then discovered that his opponent had taken five pistol shots, and over twenty slashes and stabs with a blade. Pirate chronicler Charles Johnson wrote of him that he was a "courageous brute, who might have passed in the world for a hero had he been employed in a good cause."

Blackbeard's legend by no means ends with his death however, and our thoughtful reader may still be wondering what morbid tie binds Teach's demise to the Old Burying Point. It is said, that shortly after Blackbeard's death, his head was severed from his body, and tied to the bowsprit of Maynard's ship. His body was then tossed overboard, where legend states that the mangled corpse swam three times around the sloop in the icy waters, before sinking into the turgid depths. Blackbeard's head made a tour of the Eastern Seaboard, with many clamoring to see the prize, in assurance that the Devil of piracy was indeed no more. As the years passed, the head of Blackbeard, now no more than a skull, came to rest in a tavern, where it was discovered by Edward Rowe Snow, the most famous pirate historian of all time.

He purchased the skull, which remained in his possession for many years until his death, whereupon it was bequeathed to The Peabody Essex Museum, which lies but a road's breadth away from the Old Burying Point Cemetery. The skull was donated with a caveat, written by Snow before his passing. It states that the skull may never be displayed after the sun slips below the horizon of the town where it is held. If such a contract is breached, the eyes of the skull will glow red, ghostly voices will be heard, and the city that displays it will be put under a dreadful curse. Whether or not this is true, the Museum has been thoughtful enough to never display the skull after dark.

This may not be enough to quell the rage of the pirate spectre, as multitudes have sworn that they have seen a tall figure amongst the gravestones of the ancient cemetery. A figure who appears in and out of a cloud of mist, travelling from the back of the burial ground, through the gates, and across the street to the very steps of the museum. A figure in a long grey coat with the shiniest of black buttons glinting in the streetlamps. Whether this apparition is Blackbeard or not, it is impossible to say, for the ghostly figure seen searching the gravesites he may have once walked as a mortal man, has no head.

Samuel Parris Parsonage Site:

The Salem Witchcraft Trials

65 Centre Street, Danvers

Down a dark quiet path in Salem Village, flanked by stone walls, old wooden rail fences and ancient trees, lie the timeworn stones of the Parris Parsonage cellar. It was here, in this modest site, where the Hysteria began. In the harsh winter of 1691/2 two girls in the home of the Reverend Samuel Parris began to have fits and convulsions.

His daughter Betty and his niece Abigail first showed symptoms to the family as they were discovered underneath a chair and stool, whilst twisted into odd contortions, gibbering in an unfathomable language. Abigail suffered pains in her head, and as the days went on, their symptoms became worse. Later, during examinations by the local magistrates, Tituba, an enslaved Native from South America who had travelled from the place where she was purchased in Barbados with Rev. Parris and his family, would describe the incidents in the house that led to the girls' affliction. An intelligent and resourceful woman, she would have been keenly aware of the danger she was in as soon as the girls first showed signs of illness, either mundane or supernatural, as she was their primary caretaker.

Tituba claimed that a man in black came to her bedside and told her that he would kill the girls, and her as well if she refused to aid him. A group of four women appeared in the home and forced her hands to pinch and hurt the girls, and she was approached by the Devil himself to sign her name in his book. All of these things would be told months after their supposed occurence through coercion and most likely severe beatings. It would be suggested centuries later that the girls were "learning" dark magic from Tituba, but this is never ascribed to her during her lifetime. If this were true, then the girls would have been considered "witches" themselves, and despite their young age would have been put to some questioning.

Before all this "came to light," the Parrises appealed to several doctors to find the root of the girls suffering while attempting multiple home remedies, but it was not until over a month later in February, when Dr. William Griggs suggested that the girls were "under an evil hand" that the possibility of Witchcraft came to the fore. Tituba then baked a "witch cake" with instructions from a neighbor, Mary Sibley. A witch cake was made from a flour and the afflicted's "own water" meaning their urine. The cake was then fed to a dog, with the idea that the witch attacking the girls would feel the bite of the dog's teeth and in his or her pain reveal themselves. This was the first time that the girls would have understood that they were expected to describe "who" was causing their pain, as opposed to "what."

It is important to understand that at this time, the settlers of New England were on what we would call a frontier. The area around Salem was known as the "howling wilderness" and attacks from the Natives allied with the French were common. Abigail herself was an orphan from a raid by the Abenaki which had taken her parents lives, and shortly after the first of their fits, there was a raid in York, Maine in which dozens were killed. It is our belief that what begins the Hysteria in Salem is a form of Panic Disorder brought about by PTSD. One of the other girls who is taken by fits very early on is Mercy Lewis, another orphan from the massacres in Maine.

As time goes on, the Hysteria is given legitimacy through the confessions made by Tituba Indian, which while coerced from her, are vivid and believable, and other names such as Sarah Good and Sarah Osburne are mentioned. Tituba makes reference to large meetings, in which others are described wearing black hoods and white hoods, so she cannot say who they are. Her testimonies are clear and evocative, and as spelling was not yet standardized, you can "hear" her accent in the transcriptions as when asked what the other witches command her to do, she replies, "hurt the children and last night there was an appearnce that said 'Kill the children' and if I would no go on hurtang the children they would doe worse to me." Her testimony remains remarkably consistent throughout multiple questionings.

Abigail Williams at one point described a crowd of 40 witches making communion with the blood of the afflicted in the pasture of her uncle, Samuel Parris, and she sees them hold a "Devil's Supper" inside the very home, mocking the Lord's Supper by eating bread that was like newly butchered flesh, and from goblets that surely contained a liquid too dark and ominous to be merely wine. The Hysteria spreads throughout the village, and soon old grudges begin to surface as neighbor accuses neighbor, brother accuses brother, and in at least one case, a child accuses her own mother. Over 150 people are accused, 19 men and women are hanged, one tortured to death, and several more die in prison from exposure, illness, and malnutrition.

There are books that detail the day by day accounts of the Witchcraft Trials, with Marilynne K. Roach's The Salem Witchcraft Trials being the finest example, and others that give an excellent account of the fear and wider influence of the wars with the French and Natives, such as In The Devil's Snare by Mary Beth Norton, so we will not give a full moment by moment account of the Trials here, but instead steer you in their direction.

The Hysteria and Trials are brought to their conclusion shortly after the pressing of Giles Corey (which we detail in the section on Giles Corey's Curse and the Howard Street Cemetery), and with the informal accusation of the wife of Governor William Phips, as those in power began to feel that the entire thing was being taken too far.

We would like to take a moment here to address the pervasive story about Ergot poisoning being the cause for the affliction during the Hysteria. In a study published in 1976 by Linnda Caporael, the theory is put forward mostly due to the weather conditions in the area being right for ergot to form. Ergot is a mold that grows mostly on rye, and can cause LSD-like hallucinations. While multiple people have come forward since this original study was published to disprove it, the theory remains popular, most likely because of its ability to remove culpability of those involved. The theory is extremely unlikely because of how selective it would have been to only affect certain portions of the populace, and only some within the same households. Also, all bread was served toasted, due to the belief that untoasted bread caused stomach problems, which would likely have killed off a yet further portion of the ergot that survived baking. Lastly, and most convincingly, ergot would have a necrotizing effect, and in the height of the witchcraft Hysteria, if suddenly extremities and limbs began to blacken and become beset with gangrene, it would be mentioned several times in the documents from that time, and none exist.

Samuel Parris gave his last sermon to the Salem Village Congregation on June 28th, 1696. It was discovered shortly thereafter, that as he had stated early on, he had not received proper salary payment from 1691-1695, which, especially during that particularly harsh winter of 1691/2, may have led to him having a short temper with both his children and the slaves in his household.

Though we will likely never know for certain the true cause of the Hysteria, it is far from being an attack on women or something as simple as a land grab. It is a lesson in the evils that men (and women) do to one another in times of great fear, and how what started in such a small, humble home in the darkest time of the year, can have ripples that affect humanity for centuries to come. The only pieces that remain of this home and barn where it all began, are the cellar hole stones, an eerie monument to the ghastly events that began here so long ago, and a haunting reminder of the power of fear.

The Proctor House

348 Lowell Street, Peabody

Slightly off the beaten path in the suburban pastoral area once known as Salem Farms, now the town of Peabody, sits the imposing sight of The Proctor House. The dark, somewhat foreboding structure has a bit of its grim features soothed by the modern conveniences that have been added over the years. The building is surrounded by a heavily trafficked street, other more modern buildings (and a singular chimney and fireplace, standing by itself a stone's throw away), with a swimming pool, patio, and other cheerful amenities.

Built by Thorndike Proctor, the son of the famous Witchcraft Hysteria victim John Proctor, in 1700, the interior of the house is a mishmash of centuries, with large original beams, quite possibly older than the house they now support, intersecting through rooms with replica panelling and narrow strip wood floors and modern plumbing. A fading wooden sign sits in one of the many large fireplaces, describing in brief, the history of the home, but it is far more complex than a few names and dates can entail.

John Proctor, married three times, and with a plethora of children, many lost in childbirth, was never a truly wealthy man despite inheriting land from his father in Ipswich. The land he worked in Salem Farms was about 700 acres, known as the Groton farm, rented from Emmanuel Downing, with a small home he shared with his second wife Elizabeth Thorndike, and then his third, Elizabeth Bassett. He ran, for a time, a rollicking tavern, beloved by most of his neighbors, except for the cantankerous Giles Corey.

Corey and Proctor had a contentious relationship, with numerous cases going to court. Corey once accused Proctor of selling cider to a Native in his tavern, an illegal activity during that time. Proctor in return attributed a fire that was set to his home to Corey, an action which his son later confessed to, as a careless mishap with a lantern was to blame.

During an examination of his third wife at the Salem Town Meeting House during the Witchcraft Hysteria, John Proctor was accused of witchcraft himself by John Indian, Abigail Williams, and Anne Putnam, referring to him as a "wizard," not a warlock as some modern depictions of the trials do.

A note to make here is the tendency for people to think that there was a secret relationship between Abigail Williams and John Proctor. This is purely because of Arthur Miller's "The Crucible," as in reality Abigail was only 12 at the time of the trials, and John Proctor was 60. There are no documents of any kind that suggest a relationship between them beyond accuser and accused.

A servant in the home of the Proctors, Mary Warren, a young lady, 20 years old, became one of the afflicted, and Proctor threatened to beat her if she continued to have the fits. Not long after, Warren was accused of witchcraft herself, and became one of those supposedly perpetrating the afflictions. When asked by Judge John Hathorne how it would come to pass that her role would be so changed, she calls it "a great mercy of God" to which Hathorne replies, "You take it to be a great mercy to afflict others?" Warren would later be heard in jail claiming that the afflicted did not know reality from illusion. During the examination of Alice Parker, who would later be executed, Mary Warren convulsed to the point where her tongue turned black, Parker exclaimed that Warren's tongue "would be blacker befor she dyed."

John Proctor was hanged on Gallows Hill on August 19th, 1692.

The last mention of Mary Warren is the fee for her meals in jail being crossed out in December of that year. After that, there is no further mention of Mary Warren, she vanishes, as if into thin air. Local legend states that John's body was retrieved from its shallow grave on Gallows Hill and reburied on what was the closest family land, the current site of the home his son would build less than a decade later.

Elizabeth Bassett Proctor, however, has more than her fair share of trials ahead of her in 1692 and beyond. Able to escape the hangman's noose by virtue of her pregnancy during the time of her conviction, her stepchildren have her written out of her husband's will due to the assumption that she would be later executed, and therefore was dead as far as the law was concerned, though another judge differs and grants her the original rights. The reason why Proctor's sons may have tried to maneuver Elizabeth out of her rights as a widow are unknown to us, but they would have been well-advised to remove her from their father's will at first. Under the laws of the time, the property (i.e. goods and cattle) of a convicted felon would be forfeited to the crown. Sheriff George Corwin had confiscated the property of the Proctor family already, seizing everything he and his deputies could carry from the home, even going so far as the empty out barrels of beer from the tavern so that the barrels could be sold off. Corwin took the family's entire herd of cattle, selling what cows he could and slaughtering the rest to be sold for a meager price as meat. The sons would later say the law "left nothing in the house for the support of the children." Proctor himself mourned that he and the other accused witches had their estates "undone."

Contrary to popular belief, no land was forfeited during the Hysteria of 1692. Though it would have been permitted by English law, American colonial law had long been against the practice of seizing land from felons, even in cases of witchcraft. However, a convicted or escaped witch could have their house entirely emptied of property, even down to the nails and clapboards. Perhaps the sons feared that after ransacking the home once for John's possessions, the Sheriff might return again for whatever they deemed belonged to his widow. The Sheriff had previously seized everything from convicted witch George Jacobs' widow, even pulling the wedding ring from her finger.

The Proctor House has seen only a handful of owners over the past century, and while there certainly have been joyous occasions of birth, weddings, and fresh starts within its storied frame, a hint of something ominous may be found in the shared tales of those who have lived there. One family tells a tale of falling asleep on the sofa, only to discover a quartet of candles, lit and flickering on each corner of the rug. More recent residents have complained of unusual nosebleeds, and a spectral force pushing them down the stairs. Considering the lengths to which the family of the condemned John Proctor went to keep the land he worked for decades in the hands of his descendents, it is not unlikely to think that their determination continues into the Invisible World and beyond.

The Rebecca Nurse Homestead

149 Pine Street, Danvers

Aways afield from Salem Town, inland from the harsher sea air and rocky coast, was the area known as Salem Village, now the town of Danvers. This was the less populated farming community, with a handful of small public houses, but a place where the night shadows would be keenly felt, walking or riding from the more populous areas with only your punched tin lantern and its flickering flame to drive off the darkness and unknown. It was in this community that the effects of the Witchcraft Hysteria were the most keenly felt.

Less than a mile from the Samuel Parris parsonage stands the Rebecca Nurse Homestead, and unlike many of the locations in Salem Town that are "former sites of," the Nurse Homestead is still the original structure that it was when Rebecca lived there in 1692. On March 13th of 1692, Ann Putnam Jr, daughter of Ann Carr and Thomas Putnam, had a visit from the Invisible World. Whilst staring at her grandmother's empty chair, a hazy figure of a pale woman appeared to her, seated in the chair. Her mother and their servant, Mercy Lewis questioned her repeatedly over who the spectre might be, but Ann only recognized her in the vaguest terms. Finally they were able to glean from her that she was someone who attended church at the Salem Village meeting house. Ann agreed that it must be Rebecca Nurse, who was a member of the congregation in Salem Town (located at the Rockafellas site), but due to her age, had been attending the more conveniently located sermons in Salem Village.

Rebecca Nurse was born February 21st, 1621, making her 71 years of age during the Witchcraft Hysteria. One of the oldest people accused, Rebecca was calm, and comported herself well during her first questioning, swearing that she had been at home ill for the past eight or nine days, though the afflicted (now several girls and at least three adults) writhed in agony and screamed so loudly that it startled a passerby, whenever she so much as leaned on a post to steady herself.

With nothing besides spectral evidence, because at least two adults could corroborate the visions of Nurse's spectre harming them, the magistrates Hathorne and Corwin had her sent to jail. Over the next few months, the afflicted would condemn Rebecca Nurse for multiple, horrifying offenses. The day after Nurse was jailed, Ann Putnam Jr. proclaimed that she was being bitten and lashed by a spectral chain several times over the course of a half an hour. Deacon Edward Putnam, her elderly uncle, who was in charge of the everyday tasks of church organization and attending to the poor, swore in a signed affidavit that he had seen the marks upon her, "in a kind of a round ring" at least 6 strokes across. Ann was convinced that it was Rebecca Nurse who had given her the lashing.

Constable John Putnam, cousin to Thomas, began to have fits and convulsions after idly commenting that he was not surprised that Rebecca was a witch, seeing as her mother, Joanna Towne, was a witch herself. When John and Hannah Putnam's daughter, not yet two months old, began to have convulsions that very same night, and died two days later, Rebecca Nurse was immediately suspect.

Much fault is placed on the Putnams for fanning the flames of the Hysteria, and rightly so. Between the family, dozens of people were named as possible witches. However, the reasoning behind this is very often given as a "land grab" (which we discuss as inaccurate in the chapter on The Proctor House) but it is far more likely that they are casting aspersions as widely as they can so that no accusations will fall upon them. Most of the family either held office or military rank, and were no fools. It would have been easy for them to see how those who had become "afflicted" such as Tituba and her husband John Indian, had the heat taken off of them as soon as it looked as though they were under the evil hand, and defended their family accordingly.

On June 29th, Rebecca Nurse was found innocent of the crime of witchcraft. Being generally well liked in the community, over twenty people had come to testify on her behalf, or had given written accounts to support her plea of "Not Guilty." Unfortunately, as the verdict was read out, the afflicted, which now numbered multiple girls and women, gave such a frightful cry that it chilled the officials and the jury to the marrow, causing them to reconsider their decision. They asked Rebecca a final question about a turn of phrase she had made regarding the recently condemned Mrs. Hobbs, to which she remained mute. The jury had no choice now but to return a verdict of "Guilty." It was later discovered that in all the cacophony, Rebecca, who had suffered from hearing loss for many years, had never heard the question asked of her. She was shortly thereafter excommunicated from the church congregation in the Salem Town Meeting House.

Despite at least thirty-nine people attempting to have her conviction overturned, and a temporary reprieve granted by Governor William Phips, Rebecca Nurse was hanged on July 19th 1692. It was at this execution that her fellow condemned, Sarah Good, cursed Rev. Nicholas Noyes with her last breath. "I am no more a witch than you are a wizard, and if you take away my life, God will give you blood to drink." It is said that words and conviction have power, and if the convictions behind the words of Sarah Good were supported by the other five women who stood there ready to hang, including Rebecca Nurse, then they had power indeed, for on December 13th of 1717, Noyes died of a brain hemorrhage, his mouth full of his own blood.

Two of Rebecca's sisters, Sarah Cloyce and Mary Easty, would be accused of witchcraft as well. Mary Easty was hanged months later on September 22nd, part of the last group of executions of the Trials. Her letter of appeal was considered one of the most moving ever given to a judge. She pleads, "I was confined a whole month upon the same account that I am condemned now for and then cleared by the afflicted persons as some of your honours know and in two dayes time I was cryed out upon by them and have been confined and now am condemned to die the Lord above knows my Innocence then and Likewise does now as att the great day will be know to men and Angells — I Petition to your honours not for my own life for I know I must die and my appointed time is sett but the Lord he knowes it is that if it be possible no more Innocent blood may be shed." In November of 1692, Mary Herrick would appear before Reverend Hale to report that the specter of the deceased Mary Easty and his own then still living wife's spirit had appeared before her. Mary's ghost had cried for "Vengeance, Vengeance!" and that she could only rest if her story was told and her innocence proclaimed. Sarah was released for lack of evidence, and would be portrayed centuries later by Vanessa Redgrave in the famous TV miniseries, *Three Sovereigns for Sarah*.

Rebecca Nurse, like John Proctor and all the other victims of the trials, was not given a proper burial. However, similar to Proctor, the family legend states that several of the Nurses took a small craft up the then much wider North River to Gallows Hill, and uncovered Rebecca's remains. They then brought her back to the Nurse Homestead, there to be buried under cover of darkness in her family's small grave plot. A small comfort to her loved ones, having lost their beloved matriarch, but at least she would forever rest easy on the land she once walked upon in life. This legend has later been called into question, however, as there may have been no legal reason why the family would not be able to claim their loved one's remains. We can hope that new information may be discovered, and the last resting places of other victims of the Hysteria may be found.

Many claim that Judge John Hathorne was the only one to not apologize for his role in the Trials, when in fact very few actually did. Of the Judges, only Samuel Sewall formally apologized, and a dozen of the jurymen also expressed remorse. The only one of the afflicted to give a formal apology was young Ann Putnam, whose words had condemned so many. In a letter written and read to the congregation by a relative, Ann said that she "desired to lie in the dust, and be humbled for it." Her plea is heartfelt, that she could truly say "before God and Man I did it not out of any anger, malice, or ill will towards any person" and that it was a "Great Delusion of Satan." In particular she mentions "Goodwife Nurse" and her two sisters, as a chief instrument of the accusations against them. In doing so she begged forgiveness from them, their families, and from God, for bringing upon herself and Salem "the guilt of innocent blood."

The Corwin House:
The Old Witch House

310 1/2 Essex Street, Salem

Perched on the very edge of the bustling downtown Salem district is what could easily be described as the most recognizable structure in the city, and is certainly among the most haunted.

Draped in clapboards of black, with decorations so accurately described as pendants, her stunning diamond paned casement windows winking out over the never ceasing throngs taking her picture below, the Old Witch House is a lady in her most resplendent regalia, the Queen of Salem's finest architecture and history.

Built possibly as early as the 1620s, but more likely in the 1640s, her origin is uncertain, local legends stating that the property could have belonged to Roger Williams during his early days in the Massachusetts colony, but with nothing to confirm these claims. What we do know for certain, is that Jonathan Corwin purchased it in 1675, making it the home of the Corwin family for many generations to come.

Corwin was an extremely successful merchant, improving upon the home and filling it with the most extravagant furnishings available in the colonies at that time, the structure would easily have been called a mansion in those days. He married the wealthy widow Elizabeth Gibbs, adopting her children as his own, and was, by all accounts, a well respected member of the community. He was also a member of the Colonial Assembly, and later a magistrate of the Salem courts, dealing with the petty crimes of burglary, drunkenness, and public cursing.

In 1692, Jonathan Corwin and John Hathorne, the two active magistrates in Salem Town, were asked to preside over a series of examinations that were far more serious than any crime before perpetrated in Salem. On February the 29th, possibly in the very structure we have been speaking of, four men came to complain as representatives of the community as a whole, that several girls in the Village had been afflicted with the cruelest of witchcraft, and something must be done. Corwin and Hathorne signed arrest warrants for Tituba Indian, Sarah Good, and Sarah Osborn, not knowing at the time how far or deeply the citizenry would be overwhelmed by the nearly countless accusations to follow. It would not be until late May that Governor William Phips, newly taken to the position, would set up a Court of "Oyer and Terminer," Latin for "to hear and to determine." This court was most likely suggested by his compatriot, Increase Mather, as it went along with the new Charter they were bringing to Massachusetts from England.

Due to the unbelievable numbers of the accused, and the huge area affected by the accusations, instead of setting up a Superior Court that would only be allowed to meet at specific times, this court could deal with the Witchcraft Hysteria immediately, and meet as often as needed as long as five of the nine judges were available. The season was unseasonably warm, and Phips expressed great concern for those who were suffering in the crowded and overheated jails. The court allowed "spectral evidence" which was very much the "he said she said" depictions of events, such as the "spectres" of the accused hurting the afflicted without any physical evidence. Increase Mather did not agree with spectral evidence, but his son, the famous Cotton Mather, foremost authority on Witchcraft in the Colonies at the time, believed it to be permissible.

Hathorne was placed upon the court immediately, however, there is some scholarly disagreement on how soon Corwin would be placed on the court. He may have been on from the beginning, or may not have been asked to join the court officially until Judge Nathaniel Saltonstall stepped down. What is known for certain is that he became one of the most active participants in the trials, as his home was conveniently located less than a quarter mile from where the Trials were taking place. Most of the documents that remain from the Trials show questioning either being done by Hathorne or Corwin, though the Chief Justice, William Stoughton, the current Lieutenant Governor, was the one making the most cruel of decisions, such as scheduling executions far sooner after convictions than was customary.

Even from the early days of the official Trials, there was much contention from the local community over what was perceived to be a misinterpretation of their duties. Governor Phips was very much the absentee parent of the Trials, with no record of him ever attending one himself. He was far more concerned with the ongoing attacks by the French and Abenaki tribe in his native Maine, and as early as August, during the height of the Trials, he travelled North, leaving Stoughton in charge of most Executive decisions. By the time he returned in late September, nineteen people had been executed, one man tortured to death, and hundreds still sat in jail. To make matters worse, Phips' own wife's name had been mentioned as a possible witch, and though she was never formally accused, this was more than enough to bring a terror to the households of all the previous untouchables.

Governor Phips disbanded the Court of Oyer and Terminer, and set up a new court, one that would no longer accept spectral evidence. This new court, the Court of Judicature, would be the beginnings of our current Supreme Court. Jonathan Corwin was asked to join this new court and did so, although John Hathorne was never extended an invitation. While several people were found guilty of witchcraft under this new court, there were no further executions, and eventually everyone who survived was set free, many successfully petitioning the government for reparations for family and livelihoods lost to the Hysteria. Jonathan Corwin lived for quite some time after the trials, passing away in June of 1717, just a few months shy of his 78th birthday. He lived in the house on Essex until his death, and the building stayed in the family for a few generations before becoming a boarding house, and antique store, even a pharmacy, and laundromat. In 1944, the house was scheduled to be demolished so that the street could be widened, but a group of concerned citizens came together and formed what would become Historic Salem Inc.

They purchased the home and had it moved about 35 feet back into its own property, and gave it to the city to run as a museum. A peculiar news article from this time mentions how bones were found underneath the building when it was moved, but these were very likely the remains of cows or pigs buried under the hearth after cooking. Despite this knowledge, to this day tours in Salem will tell the false tale of a witch buried under the home, or other, wilder tortures performed there in Judge Corwin's time, all of which, we can assure you, carry no basis in fact.

The Witch House has had the name since at least the 1800s, purely for its owner being involved in the Trials and likely thanks to the entrepreneurial spirit of George Farrington, whose pharmacy sold medicine in bottles branded with a flying witch on a broomstick. Today it is the only structure in Salem Town with a direct historical connection to the Trials.

Despite it not having any dark, disturbing history, save for the usual high infant mortality rate of the Colonial era, there are more diverse eyewitness accounts of hauntings here than anywhere else in the city. It was, in fact, one of the first locations of ghost photography, when in 1897, photographer Walter Sprange caught a spectral cat on film that he described as "one of the most woe-begotten, ill-shaped cats" peeking out of the casement window and then the doorway.

The famous master of macabre literature, H.P. Lovecraft, was so fascinated by the eldritch structure that he set one of his deepest delves into the supernatural in it. "The Dreams in The Witch House" was written in 1932, and while the supposed "witch" of the story is a fabrication, the description of the fears of the Witchcraft Hysteria and testimonies of the afflicted, as well as the portions describing the house itself in the late 1920s are quite accurate. Though the House in the story is torn down, in so doing they discover the skeletons of countless children in a room above the eaves, this was written before the bones were discovered beneath the hearth, making Lovecraft's tale the likely reason why so many people believe the story of bodies buried there.

We ourselves worked at The Witch House for many years, and have had many first hand accounts of ghostly activity. One early morning, two ladies came in from the rain the day after Halloween, and as they were being told about those executed during the Trials, a tin candle sconce hurled itself with such force from its place hanging on the wall, that it struck the opposite side. The guests whirled around at the loud noise and stared in shock at the sconce and red candle rolling along the floor. Odd shadows that move like people will appear and disappear around the attic, long after the house is closed, and a spectral presence in the eaves has frightened more than one guide to the point that they would no longer enter it unaccompanied. In fact, at least one person working at the house was so frightened of it that she never entered the structure proper, only the gift shop and offices in the later added lean-to.

Many children will swear they have visited the house before, and accurately describe the upstairs children's room without ever setting foot in it, claiming it was "their house." Many have claimed to see a woman in a long orange skirt heading up the stair, only to arrive at the second floor and find it empty. The most unbelievable ghost encounter I, the writer, have ever had in all my years running ghost tours and living in ancient houses, occurred one otherwise unremarkable morning at the Corwin House.

There used to be a very large sign that wrapped around the wooden pillar out front, and that particular morning, after I had maneuvered it outside, I returned to the house to slide the bolt in for the massive front door. After I did so, I saw a figure in a grey greatcoat, with a powdered wig and tricorn hat in the room that we call the kitchen, or "hall." The figure was facing away from me, having a heated conversation with themselves, though I could not hear them or see anyone else in the room. At the time, I assumed that what I was seeing was a coworker who gave historic tours in full costume, and would often begin them at the house. I called out a greeting to them, but was unsurprised to receive no response, as they were obviously deeply engaged in rehearsing their tour, or so I thought. Leaving them to their rehearsal I went to see the director of the home, and asked idly about our coworker's tour. She gave me a puzzled look, and informed me that she had no idea that he was going to be in that day, and she certainly hadn't heard him come in. Feeling a cold chill run up my spine I informed her that no one had passed me, or I absolutely would have seen them, or heard the massive front door unlatch. After a moment where we both stared at each other, frozen, we dashed into the house, certain that someone had somehow snuck in around us. Of course when we reached the kitchen there was not a living soul to be found, and whatever apparition I had seen was gone as well.

The Joshua Ward House:
George Corwin

148 Washington Street, Salem

We say of many locations in Salem that the truth is stranger than the fiction, and as such, there is no need to create stories about any of the sites that we mention in this book, the truth is what is so fascinating. While we may say a particular story is "local legend" we will gladly inform you of when the legend is without any grains of truth. When it comes to the Ward house, often called the "Most Haunted House in Salem," the fiction may be stranger than the truth, even if the truth is, by itself, extremely unsettling.

Built in 1784 for one of Salem's many successful merchant sea captains, Joshua Ward, with interiors designed by master architect Samuel McIntire, it is truly one of the gems of the Federal style buildings of its era. George Washington himself insisted that of all the homes that had invited him to stay when he visited Salem in 1789, the one he desired to stay at the most was the Ward House. Today the mansion is known as The Merchant Inn, and guests are still enamored with the luxurious craftsmanship that may be found throughout the hotel.

It is not Joshua Ward and his magnificent home that gives the site such a prominent place in ghostly accounts of Salem however, but the owner of the land in 1692 during the height of the Witchcraft Hysteria, none other than the notorious Sheriff George Corwin. George Corwin, nephew of the magistrate and judge, Jonathan Corwin, was perhaps the most villainous character of that woebegone era. His crimes are multitude; theft of property, torture, even murder, most protected by the new English charter of the Massachusetts Bay Colony, that had heretofore forbade such acts as illegal.

John Proctor wrote a plea to several gentlemen of the Boston courts stating that the treatment of George Corwin and the magistrates against numerous people, including his son, William Proctor, were appalling. He described his son being tied neck and heels, think hog-tied, with a rope around your neck as well, that strangled you if you struggled, as he said, "til the Blood gushed out at his Nose" and would have been left that way for 24 hours had a cooler head not intervened. He describes the tortures as similar to "popish cruelties," most likely a reference to a small book published in London in 1680, called "A Scheme of Popish Cruelties or A Prospect of what we must expect under a Popish successor." This was filled with incredibly lewd and evocative illustrations of the horrors one could expect under a Pope of the Roman Catholic church, a propaganda piece that would have been very familiar, and a stern warning to the Puritans of the day. Proctor's letter was reviewed by eight Bostonian ministers, who eventually reversed their stance on the allowance of spectral evidence against the accused, but it was too little too late to save John Proctor.

Some misinformed people will claim that Corwin had a private torture dungeon somewhere on his property, but the sad truth of the matter is that his tortures could be played out publicly in the Salem Gaol, as none of his actions were illegal under the Massachusetts Charter. William Proctor was certainly not the only person to suffer at the hands of George Corwin, as his actions during the pressing of Giles Corey (See Howard Street/The Curse of Giles Corey) are particularly heinous and abhorrent, and his infamous relationship with Phillip English (See St. Peter's Church) was the stuff of legends.

Many wonder why someone as young as George was during the trials (25) was given such power and authority. Nepotism was certainly as common during the Witchcraft Hysteria as it is today, and George's great-grandfather was none other than John Winthrop, the founder of Boston, first governor of the Massachusetts Bay Colony. Winthrop Sr. was the man whose Puritan ideal of a "city upon a hill" was meant to be the shining example of all that was good, and stand against the evils of the New World and beyond. It is unfortunate that his descendant's name would forever be synonymous with the most unspeakable crimes of Massachusetts' darkest days.

The origin of the ghostly tales at the Ward House may come from an often misinterpreted legend involving Corwin. There are many who believe that George's bones are hidden somewhere on the property, having been placed amidst the stones of the cellar to keep his body safe from theft. While this counters the story Philip English's family has told, and George is now safely interred in the Broad Street Cemetery (as far as we can tell) one can easily see why people would latch on to such a ghoulish tale. Edgar Allen Poe has a deep connection with Salem, and his tales "The Black Cat" and "The Cask of Amontillado" both involve an unfortunate soul being bricked up into the walls of a cellar, which was not an uncommon place to hide an inconvenient corpse, and along with the sensationalization of the bones discovered at the Witch House/Corwin House, may have helped keep the salacious rumor alive. Whether George was a temporary occupant of the cellar or no, we can all but guarantee that it is not his eternal resting place.

There are multiple eerie accounts from locals and tourists that have visited the site over the years. You can talk with lifelong residents of Salem who worked in the area during the time when there were shops built around the front about their experiences with lights turning on and off, disembodied voices echoing from empty rooms, almost your textbook haunted house experiences. There have been visits more recently where people claim to have felt spectral hands grasping at their throats, and certainly these are stories that we can neither confirm, nor deny.

The ghostly photo that gives the structure the moniker of "Most Haunted Home in Salem" however, is one of the easiest ghost photos to discredit. Some say that one of the most frightening ghost photos ever taken is that of a cursed "witch," the unfortunate victim of Sheriff George Corwin, who cannot rest easy, and stalks the hallways of the Ward House. We are sorry to disappoint anyone, but the famous photo of "the Witch of the Ward House" is nothing more than a person at a Christmas party, who happened to be standing in front of a particularly large wreath. The lady in the picture is absolutely aware of the photo's infamy, and is more than a little embarrassed by it, so we have chosen not to print it here, out of respect to her and her family.

This is not to say that there is no evidence of hauntings there, and we ourselves have had our fair share of chills when walking past the stately mansion at night, as though there were figures from the Invisible World peering at us from the imposing structure. There is no need to manufacture a ghost in Salem, when they seem to be lurking just around every corner...

Rockafellas:
The Salem Town Meeting House

231 Essex Street, Salem

R ockafellas may be the only place in town where you can have a drink with a ghost, or, at the very least, have a drink named after one. The phantom "Lady in Blue" may be the most famous ghost in Salem you have never heard of, though the site the building stands on is host to numerous macabre tales that connect to the Witchcraft Hysteria, Nathaniel Hawthorne, and one of Salem's first purveyors of the tourist trade.

The current building still bears the faded name of its most famous owner, high above the patrons who sit out on the patio enjoying hearty fare and cocktails. Daniel Low & Co. began as a single rented room, humble jewelry shop of the workaholic Daniel Low. In 1891, Low created what would become one of Salem's first, and truly unique souvenirs; a delicate silver spoon graced with an elegant witch and pins, engraven with the city's name. The spoons were an instant success, later becoming more elaborate, adding a small cat and broom, and soon Daniel Low had created the world's first mail order catalog to keep up with the demand. His business expanded to the point where he took over the entire first floor of the building, and had tunnels widened beneath the building to accommodate the movement of goods to his warehouse next door without the need to go outside in inclement weather. Daniel Low's success was sadly to be short lived.

On February 3rd of 1911, Low dropped dead on the floor of his business, victim to his lifetime of overwork. The Daniel Low & Co. business was finally closed for good in 1994, and since the building's conversion to a restaurant in the early 2000s, servers have experienced a startling array of paranormal phenomena. Chairs stacked up for the evening would all be neatly placed below their tables again mere moments later, random objects would suddenly go missing, and every salt shaker in the building would suddenly vanish after everyone had left for the evening. A bartender tells the story of a glass completely exploding in front of his very eyes, and a multitude of eerie occurrences have taken place in the tunnels below the building. Freezers will close by themselves, and emit a knocking sound when no one is inside. Blonde women will swear that they have been pushed while standing on a certain step, or in the case of this author, feel a comforting hand caressing her shoulder within a single minute of visiting the basement of the building, only to find no one behind them.

The site of the current building is extremely close to where the meeting house stood in 1692. Just across the street from the home of John Hathorne, it was in this second meeting house that the First Congregation of Salem met, including several of the most famous names from Salem Village. Rebecca Nurse, John and Elizabeth Proctor, and Giles Corey all attended church in this building, and each was eventually excommunicated there. The Governor's Council held several of its investigations there, as the building, though greatly in need of repair, was much larger and more spacious than the Salem Town House where the Trials were held, just a few hundred feet away. It was here that John Proctor was first accused by Abigail Williams and Anne Putnam, as they swore they saw Elizabeth Proctor's spirit dancing madly on the wooden beams. Shortly thereafter, they would accuse John of being the mastermind behind it all, and the following day claim that his spirit was sitting in the laps of the members of court. John Indian even exclaimed that he could see Proctor riding Rev. Parris' dog.

Bridget Bishop also has a bitter connection to the Meeting House that once stood in the square. In 1677 she was accused and convicted of cursing her husband Thomas Oliver as an "Old Rogue" and "Old Devil" on the Sabbath day. She and her husband were sentenced to stand back to back in the meeting house square by the town pump, their mouths gagged, their crime of arguing on the Sabbath pinned to their caps. In the end it was only Bridget who was forced to bear the weight of this hour of humiliation, as her stepdaughter, Mary West, paid her father's fee, relieving him of the public's scorn, and Bridget stood alone. It was in this very spot, 15 years later, that an errant glance to the old meeting house would prove to be her undoing. As she cast her eyes towards the building, there was a tremendous crash from inside, and upon inspection, a massive board studded with nails was found to have tumbled down to the floor, causing the cacophony within. It was this event that solidified the public opinion, that despite being found innocent of Witchcraft charges a decade prior, Bridget Bishop was indeed a witch.

Just outside Rockafellas, the town pump is now represented by a bronze and stone fountain, artistically depicting the history of Salem and surrounded by concrete blocks carved with the words of a cautionary tale by Nathaniel Hawthorne, "A Rill from the Town Pump." Written in 1837 as part of his collection of short stories, Twice Told Tales, the Pump speaks to the town, foreseeing an age when liquor, tea, and other such drinks will be cast aside in favor of the pure water which it provides. In a cleverly prophetic line it proclaims, "And, when I shall have decayed, like my predecessors, then, if you revere my memory, let a marble fountain, richly sculptured, take my place upon this spot. " It may not be a marble, but a fountain it is indeed, and as the words of Hawthorne tease us as they did almost a century ago, it is delightful to think that they look out across the street at the land which once belonged to his great-great grandfather.

Rockafellas casts a large shadow on this storied corner, both literally and figuratively, and while it has seen many illustrious comings and going over the years, its most famous haunting is related to neither Daniel Low, nor the Witchcraft Hysteria, or even Nathaniel Hawthorne. Over the decades, a mysterious lady in a sky blue dress has been seen both inside and outside the building, appearing as a full apparition to terrified viewers, and as a spectral form in photographs. There are many tales as to her origin, some connecting her to another spectre that roams the upper Colonial Hall banquet rooms, a mysterious minister who supposedly hanged himself in the area that was once a church. The most pervasive story as to her origin is that during one of the many times the building was demolished and reconstructed, either scraps of a blue dress, an entire blue dress, or even a body in a blue dress was discovered, bricked up in the walls. Perhaps she was the mistress of the ghostly minister who is seen angrily storming through the rooms reserved for the new couples celebrating their union in Colonial Hall, jealous of the happiness that those trapped in the Invisible World will never be able to experience themselves.

The Lyceum Hall:
Bridget Bishop

43 Church Street, Salem

W arm candlelight flickers behind shining window panes as glasses clink and murmured conversation and laughter spill out onto the brick walkways behind the old Lyceum building. The air is heavy with the delicious wafting smell of seafood, and maybe, just maybe, you will catch a whiff of apples.

The Lyceum in its heyday was the place to be for attending lectures from the most notable names of the time when they came to visit Salem. Built by the Salem Lyceum Society in 1831, the imposing brick structure would have been filled with the elite of society who came to hear such notable names as Ralph Waldo Emerson, Frederick Douglass, John Quincy Adams and Henry David Thoreau speak. The site was also a common location for the demonstrations of new technology and inventions in the hopes of gaining investors.

In 1877, Alexander Graham Bell made a call to Boston on his new device, the telephone, much to the astonishment of the assembled personage, though he was unable to convince a single investor, because why would anyone want to use that when they could just send a telegraph? Bell may have been ahead of his time, but considering the preference of text messages today, his investors may have been ahead even further.

One of the most intriguing events held at the Lyceum was the dumb supper, an event where groups of people, often several from a family, would be seated for a plated meal, with an empty setting between every set of guests, specifically for those that had passed on. The meal would be eaten without a word spoken, hoping that the members of the Invisible World would join them for their silent feast. Apart from this event, there were no reports of ghostly activity in the Hall until many years later.

The apparitions attributed to this site may not be related in any way to the salad days of the Lyceum, but instead the original settler of the land, Bridget Bishop. Bridget Bishop, 60 years of age at the time of her execution, had been married three, or possibly four times, and was by all accounts an outspoken and spirited woman. Bishop would, through numerous accusations, be convicted of witchcraft, and be the very first person to hang for it.

The property on what is now Church Street belonged to her late husband, Thomas Oliver. Upon the land, she and her new husband Edward Bishop had a home and ran the small apple orchard which she had grown with Thomas. It is perhaps because of this that people swear they smell the sun-warmed fresh scent of ripening apples while walking past the Lyceum, no matter the time of year. It was in this orchard that John Louder, who was working at the Ship's Tavern around the corner on what is now the Essex Pedestrian Mall, witnessed a horrific sight that would be one of many nails in the figurative coffin of Bridget Bishop.

Louder, who had stayed home sick from afternoon Sabbath service, discovered a jet black pig in the locked tavern, and as shocked as he was by this discovery, what happened next would cause him to lose the ability to speak for three days. A creature of the devil; an imp, appeared suddenly from an open window. The creature had the face of the man, but a body like a monkey, covered in black fur, with the feet of a chicken. It came to him and promised all forms of earthly delights, but he swore that he denied it by pronouncing, "The whole armor of God is between me and you!" While this terrifying encounter was taking place, he witnessed Bridget Bishop (then Oliver) out in her apple orchard. When he was finally able to chase away the fiend, it flew towards her in the orchard, scattering apples in its wake.

This was far from the only account against Bishop, in fact there seemed to be fewer people who had not seen her perform an act of witchcraft than those who had. Her powers seemed to be all encompassing, from tossing people down riverbanks or about their own yards, causing all manner of incurable diseases, convulsions, and fits, to coins that she had given in payment disappearing into thin air. Most salaciously, many men would claim to have seen her appear in their bedchambers at night, wearing the bright red bodice that she became famous for.

Jonathan Walcott was said to have slashed at Bridget Bishop's spectre with his sheathed sword as it attacked his sister Mary, and they had heard the fabric tear. When Bishop was inspected, a tell-tale rip was found on her skirt. This was accepted as physical evidence against her. A note here is the difficulty in discussing the many afflictions caused by Bridget Bishop, in that there was a Sarah Bishop also in the town, and it is more than possible that some of these tales ascribed to Bridget may not have been claims against her at all.

Bridget would hang for the crime of witchcraft in Salem, brought by cart to the area now known as Proctor's Ledge, and hanged on either a temporary gallows or convenient tree, over the salt marsh pools at a turn of the North River on June 10th, 1692. The witnesses were numerous, and even at her execution new crimes were placed on her, as the presiding minister heard a local man claim that she had bewitched his child to death, and he would not pray for her damned soul. The site itself has been in contention for many years, but we have several accounts that have led scholars to the present location. President John Adams himself visited the site in 1766, as he attests in his memoirs, "walked to Witchcraft hill, a hill about half a mile from Cranch's, where the famous persons formerly executed for witches were buried. Somebody within a few years has planted a number of locust trees over the graves, as a memorial of that memorable victory over the 'prince of the power of the air.' This hill is in a large common belonging to the proprietors of Salem, & c. From it you have a fair view of the town, of the river, the north and south fields, of Marblehead, of Judge Lynde's pleasure-house, & c. of Salem Village, &c."

Of Bridget Bishop's home, there is not a trace left, save for the supposed lingering scent of apples, and a persistent haunting of the Old

Lyceum building where it once stood. One of the most investigated buildings in Salem, countless ghostly photos and supernatural experiences have been recorded therein. Often a mysterious figure is seen walking up and down the stairs to the event halls on the second floor, and technology has an odd way of communicating messages that seem to come from the Invisible World.

Most convincingly, is the common occurrence of people complaining of a heavy weight upon their shoulders, or tripping over an unseen obstacle as they pass by the building while walking down Church Street, or along the sidewalk that connects to Federal Street. It must be noted, that though very rarely does someone know the history while walking this path, this is the same journey each convicted victim of the trials would have taken to the Salem Gaol, their hands and feet bound by chain, either conveyed by cart, or forced to take their final steps of freedom. Bridget Bishop herself would have had one last glimpse of her home and orchard that she treasured so dearly, as she was sent to Gallows Hill.

The Old Salem Gaol

10 Federal Street, Salem

Nothing remains of the infamous Salem Gaol, save for a small plaque upon the brick edifice that signifies where it once stood, and a single beam that rests in a place of prominence on the wall in the Witch Dungeon Museum (the site that bears the original plaque, but not the original location). In its day, the small county prison was full to bursting with the wretched condemned and those awaiting further trial during the Witchcraft Hysteria of 1692, and though the structure may be long gone, the souls of those poor, ill-fated, piteous masses may still be bound to the earth that they were shackled to in life.

The gaol was built in 1684 to serve as the county seat prison, so while slightly larger than others from that time, its two story framework was never intended to deal with the massive amount of people who were accused, and thusly it would often serve as an interim prison as the accused were passed from location to location across the North Shore and Boston, some going up as far as the much smaller Ipswich jail. The prisons were at times so crowded that there was reportedly not even enough space to lay down, and the accused would be forced to stand for days at a time.

The prisoners would be bound to the floor with hard iron shackles, the belief being that the iron would serve as a ward against their spirits attacking the afflicted. Perhaps this comes from the idea that iron, or more specifically "cold iron" was a powerful repellent of fairies, ghosts, and witches. Saint Dunstan, once the Archbishop of Canterbury, who lived in the 900s, was said to have nailed a horseshoe to the foot of the Devil himself when the Prince of Lies asked him to reshoe his horse. The bit of iron caused him such pain that when Dunstan promised to remove it only if he agreed to never set foot in a house which hung a horseshoe upon the threshold, the Devil was quick to strike the bargain. Poppets or Witch Bottles full of iron nails would often be placed in walls as traps to protect the home against evil spirits. Supernatural confinements aside, the prison was a hellish place.

The summer was broiling to the point that the Governor showed concern for the imprisoned, but it was the winter, with its frigid winds that made the gaol a deadly place for the young and infirm. Illnesses and pests were rampant, infecting dozens at a time. Several people did not survive the torment of the prison system, and at least one perished within the Salem Gaol's walls. Ann Foster, seventy five years of age from Andover died after twenty one weeks in prison. Her family later successfully fought to have the fees incurred by her incarceration reimbursed. In the Boston jail, Sarah Osborne, one of the first accused, died of exposure and malnutrition, and Roger Toothaker, a noted local witch-finder and untrained physician who claimed his daughter had once killed a witch, died after only a month's time incarcerated. Lydia Dustin would be found not guilty of witchcraft in February 1693, but was unable to pay her jailer's fee, and died in the Cambridge Jail the following month. Sarah Good's infant child would also become a victim of the deadly nature of the prisons. It was from the Salem Gaol that Giles Corey was taken to "a nearby field" to be tortured until death by peine forte et dure.

The prison saw several structural changes over the years, and it finally closed for operation in 1813, when the Salem Jail was built next to the Howard Street Cemetery. The timbers of the old gaol were repurposed into a family home in 1863 by Abner Cheney Goodall, the descendent of the same family as Jacob Goodall, the manservant that was murdered by Giles Corey. In the 1930s, the Goodall family decided to open the first salem "Witch Attraction," a facsimile of the gaol that once stood upon the property.

In 1956, the building was completely demolished by the New England Telephone Company, and their new office building, which is what currently stands in that location, was built shortly thereafter. From day one of the construction of this building there have been numerous accounts of ghostly activity, especially from employees who had the misfortune to be there after dark. One particularly frightening tale is of an employee working late one evening, when the lights started to turn off all around him, one by one, until he was alone in the darkness. Or was he? He could hear someone getting closer and closer to him amidst the empty cubicles, but as he called out, there was no reply. As the feeling of another person drew near, he swore he could hear someone breathing faintly, and a sound like the dragging of a chain. After what felt like an eternity, he felt the brush of a cold hand upon his shoulder, he let out a scream and the lights flickered back on. He found himself completely alone, not a single living soul around. The employee quit the following day, never to return.

The site is so famous for its hauntings that it is not uncommon to see a group of paranormal investigators outside the building all through October, and we have even witnessed a group of men out in the parking lot next to the building attempting a guerilla exorcism of the site! Whatever remains in that plot of land, it is tenacious, for stories of hauntings still occur there to this day. If you stand outside late at night, you too may have the fortune (or misfortune), of meeting one of the spirits that linger there yourself!

The Gardner-Pingree and Crowninshield-Bentley Houses:

The Murder of Captain White

129 and 126 Essex Street, Salem

The Gardner-Pingree House looms over the east end of Essex Street, shaded by two great hundred-year-old trees. The mansion is as mysterious as it is beautiful and holds a gruesome secret that would inspire some of the greatest minds in gothic horror to weave tales around it that might pale in comparison to the truly horrid history. When famed architect Samuel McIntire designed this home in 1805 for merchant John Gardner, perhaps he would have put his plans in the fireplace had he known what sort of man might live in that house, and what horror would occur within its walls.

In 1830, the home belonged to Captain Joseph White, a merchant with numerous ships at sea and a vast fortune in the bank. Known throughout Salem as one of its most successful privateers during the Revolutionary War, the Captain was also involved in a far more unsavory profession; the trading of human slaves. He had been involved in this odious trade for quite some time, and his ship the Felicity had chartered many a poor victim from Africa to their new lives of forced servitude. A slave revolt on the Felicity in 1789 caused the death of one of one his captains; no report remains on with what deadly force this uprising may have been put down. White himself had once told the Reverend William Bentley that he was not troubled by his barbaric profession at all, saying he had "no reluctance selling any member of the human race."

The Captain's word was respected by the community, however, he didn't seem to care much for anyone and kept out of local matters unless he felt directly involved. Within his family there was a great deal of resentment toward the old man. The Captain had no children, and his wife had died many years before. At eighty years of age, the Captain decided to change his will completely and greatly favor his nephew Stephen White, a wealthy politician, over the family of his niece Mary Beckford, who was a maid in the Captain's home. This situation became even worse when Beckford's daughter Mary White Beckford, whom the Captain had great affection for, professed her love for Joe Knapp Jr, an employee of the Captain's. Captain White accused Knapp of trying to get his hands on his fortune. He warned the lovers that if they were married, they would regret it. Immediately after the two were married, the Captain fired Joe Knapp and the newly named Mary White Knapp was disinherited and cut out of his will completely.

The night of April 6th, 1830, the Captain retired to his bed around nine thirty. The house was emptier than usual that night. Mary Beckford was gone to visit her daughter at her farm in Wenham, so only the upstairs maid Lydia and the handyman, his distant relative Benjamin White, were at home. They both slept in servant's quarters far away from the Captain's room.

The Captain walked up to his bedroom, blowing out all of the candles as he went, for he cared not to have any light in the house at night. The last candle would have been blown out at his bedside. Perhaps an hour later, Daniel Bray, whose home was set behind the Captain's on Brown Street, saw a suspicious man keeping to the shadows and trying to avoid detection. Something about the man told Bray that he was up to no good. Bray approached a neighbor, John Southwick, who said he too had seen the stranger, who now lurked in the shadows next to Bray's house.

Both men hid on the second floor of Bray's house to keep watch on him. There was a menacing, dreadful air about this man, and Bray was fearful of making any noise, lest he catch the man's attention. A short while later, another man approached the first. They spoke briefly, then each quickly fled in opposite directions. One of the men ran down Howard Street. The second man had come down a path that would have meant he had just left the back of the home of Captain White.

The following morning, Benjamin White awoke and walked to the kitchen of the mansion. He noticed the back window was open, and a wooden plank put up to it. Alarmed, he raced upstairs to check on the Captain and found his normally-closed door wide open. Once approached the room and peered inside, Benjamin gasped with horror. The Captain lay dead in his bed, the side of his head caved in by the crush of a single, powerful blow. He had thirteen stab wounds in his body, all aimed at his heart. Nothing had been stolen from the home. The locked iron chest at the foot of the Captain's bed was undisturbed. The murderer had stolen nothing except for the Captain's life.

The eye of suspicion naturally fell on the old man's family. Under the new will, Captain's three nieces would inherit $25,000 each, and Stephen White would inherit up to $200,000 and the mansion. When it was learned that he would inherit the majority of the Captain's fortune, Stephen found himself grabbed by the collar and shaken by his brother-in-law. Fearful that he would be dragged into a charge of murder from his own family, Stephen knew he had best try to get to the bottom of the story himself. He helped to create a Committee of Vigilance; the well-to-do and inquisitive merchants of Salem became amatuer crime sleuths whose activities were funded by Stephen White. He gave permission for the autopsy report to be published, and soon, the shadow of this mysterious killing quickly spread across the state and eventually, the country.

Every newspaper in America ran the story of the murder of Captain Joseph White; the wealthy old man brutally killed in his bed by an unknown assailant. Newspapers ran the gory details of the murder, claiming that telling the whole story was the only way to help the police capture the criminal before he struck again. The Rhode Island American editorial summed up the sensational outcry over this crime by stating Salem is "forever stained with blood, blood, blood!"

In time, the murderers' secrets would come to light. They had been careful to cover their tracks, but not careful enough. They had been careless and left clues and witnesses behind. A letter arrived at the home of Joseph Knapp Sr, demanding money in exchange for the nondisclosure of certain plans about the time of April 2. Unsure of the letters meaning, he brought it to his son, the aforementioned Joseph Jr, who told him it was "a devilish lot of trash" and told him to turn the letter in to the Committee. The group cornered the letter-writer, a petty thief whose statements ironically lead them right back to the intended recipient of his letter, Joseph Knapp Jr.

After Joe Kapp Jr was fired by the Captain and his young wife disinherited of her future, Joe and his brother Frank had chosen to drink away their sorrows one night, and then hit upon a comforting thought that would begin them on their bloody course. They supposed that if the newly-written will of the Captain was to go missing, then upon his death, the law would force the old man's fortune to be split up equally between his heirs, or at the very least, the previous will would need to be adhered to in the event the first was lost. Joe devised of how he might steal the Captain's will from the iron-clad trunk in his bedroom. This all relied on a very important and ghastly part of their plan; Captain White had to die.

The brothers thought about the best way to murder the old man, but realized neither of them truly had the courage to carry out the crime… but Frank knew someone who did. Richard Crowninshield was a desperate man with a long history of trouble and crime. Frank was acquainted with Richard and his brother George from several years before when the trio stole three hundred dollars from Frank's father to get them New York City and begin their new lives as thieves; which abruptly ended when they were arrested, jailed and returned home.

Several meetings took place between the Knapp brothers and the Crowninshield boys, and eventually Richard agreed to take on the deadly job for a fee of one thousand dollars. Richard and George were arrested when a man came forward and claimed to have been in a Salem gambling-house where he overheard the brothers talking about stealing the iron chest from Captain White's room. Joe and Frank Knapp were arrested not long after the blackmail letter was received by the committee; prompted by Joe himself, of course. This was one of many errors in judgment Joe Knapp made during this time.

An associate of Captain White's, Reverend Henry Coleman, convinced Joe Jr. that if he confessed to the crime and blamed the murder on the Crowninshields, he and his brother would be safe from prosecution. Joe took the Reverend at his word and signed his name to a nine-page confession. When he was told that Joe had confessed, Frank grew angry and admitted to hiding the murder weapons; a lead-tipped bludgeon and a five-inch dirk, under the steps of the church on Howard Street. This left

Richard and George in a very precarious position. Richard had built the bludgeon himself, and the dirk belonged to George; a weapon he had often casually displayed and even jokingly poked his friends with. They were both most definitely tied to those instruments of murder. Richard believed that since he would undoubtedly be charged as the principal, if he were not convicted, the accessories could not be convicted either. He likely cared little for the fates of the Knapps, but would have wanted to protect his brother from the hangman's noose.

Richard decided that he would have the last laugh on the authorities who were so eager to convict him for murder, and the public who cried out to see him hanged before the eyes of the world. He hanged himself in his jail cell, leaving notes for his father and brother, but confessing to nothing. His suicide, however, was all the confession needed by the special prosecutor Daniel Webster. The famed attorney, lawmaker and orator handled the case that was now presented against Frank Knapp as the principal, since only Frank could be tied to the actual site of the murder. It was he who had hidden in the shadows of Daniel Bray's home.

With his gift for skillful prose, Webster painted the scene of the murderous plot executed by the Knapps and Crowninshields, and took the jury through Richard's steps that fateful night: "The assassin enters, through the window already prepared, into an unoccupied apartment. With noiseless foot he paces the lonely hall, half lighted by the moon. He winds up the ascent of the stairs and reaches the door of the chamber. Of this he moves the lock, by soft and continued pressure, till it turns on its hinges, and he enters, and beholds his victim before him. The room was uncommonly open to the admission of light. The face of the innocent sleeper was turned from the murderer, and the beams of the moon, resting on the gray locks of his aged temple, showed him where to strike. The fatal blow is given, and the victim passes, without a struggle or a motion, from the repose of sleep to the repose of death! It is the assassins' purpose to make sure work, and he yet plies the dagger, though it was obvious that life had been destroyed by the blow of the bludgeon. He even raises the aged arm, that he may not fail in his aim at the heart, and replaces it again over the wounds of the poniard! To finish the picture, he explores the wrist for the pulse! He feels it, and ascertains that it beats no longer! It is accomplished. The deed is done. He retreats, retraces his steps to the window, passes out through it as he came in, and escapes. He had done the murder. No eye has seen him; no ear has heard him. The secret is his own, and it is safe!"

In the end, though it took two trials (the first ended in a deadlocked jury) Frank Knapp was convicted for the murder of Captain Joseph White. Tears rolled down the cheeks of Judge Samuel Putnam as he pronounced the sentence on the twenty-year-old Knapp, to be taken "from thence to the place of execution, there to be hanged by the neck until you are dead."

Frank stared at the judge with a cold, unflinching emotionless gaze as the sentence of death fell upon him. Joe Knapp Jr. would not see that promised immunity, and refused to testify before the court, against the counsel of his attorney. He too, would be sentenced to death. The Knapp boys were hanged together at the Salem Jail. However, Richard's attempt to save the life of his brother was successful. With no way to tie him to the site of the murder, George would be found 'not guilty' and walk out of the courtroom a free man. He would never get his dirk back, however, it is to this day in the possession of the Peabody Essex Museum, along with the bludgeon.

John and Frank Knapp are buried in the Howard Street Cemetery, and share that resting place with the very man whose life they took, Captain White. The murder mystery came to a close, but a new chapter opened not long after. The home was believed to be cursed due to the awful murder, and some wondered if the old Captain may not still walk the halls, reliving the night of his murder. In the evening hours, it is said the Captain returns to the home. The ancient man's ghost is said to walk the house, going from one room to another. He will most often be seen in his bedroom, which has four windows to it; two facing Essex Street and two facing to the west where the Essex Heritage Society building sits beside it. The furnishings within the building are not the Captain's own, but perhaps he still considers the home to be his. If, as the legend goes, he is reliving that terrible night over and over, perhaps it is poetic justice for a man who mercilessly sent so many into a lifetime of slavery.

The haunting may even spread outside of the home, in what is now the front yard of the Crowninshield-Bentley House. The home was moved to its present location in the 1960s, but the property it sits on was owned by Captain White. The spectral form of an elderly man clad in a black suit with black spectacles has been seen walking this property, thought strangely only children seem to be able to see it. Children will see the ghost and describe it in detail while adults look on the same site and see nothing. Throughout the history of Witch Trials, children have been relied upon to see the Invisible World that adults are blind to, for children are "untainted with sin." The fact that only children can see the ghost may point to the truth of this belief, or perhaps an unknown soft spot in the Captain for children, since he certainly seemed to have no love for any adult he knew.

The fame of this murder lives on in the works of most famous writers of the day. Nathaniel Hawthorne had a front-row seat for the unfolding of this mystery, and had written in a letter that he thought little of Joe, but hoped that Frank would not hang. His 1834 short story "Mister Higgenbotham's Catastrophe" shows signs of mimicking the uproar that swept through Salem's residents with every turn of events, though it has a much happier ending. H.P. Lovecraft would set his chilling tale of human possession, "The Thing On The Doorstep" at the Crowninshield house, which sees a murder committed by a single blow to the head.

Another who found inspiration in this dreadful murder was Edgar Allan Poe. His story of cold-blooded and cruel murder "The Tell Tale Heart" clearly wears its influence from the jury summation of Daniel Webster. It is not hard to hear Poe's story of a murderer drawn into complete madness by his own guilt in Webster's words. The killer imagines the sound of the beating heart of the vulture-eyed old man he has murdered, certain everyone knows his guilt, until he can take no more and confesses his crime. This is especially true when reading Webster's passage on the effect of murder on one's own conscience; "The human heart was not made for the residence of such an inhabitant... A vulture is devouring it, and it can ask no sympathy or assistance, either from heaven or earth. The secret which the murderer possesses soon comes to possess him... He feels it beating at his heart, rising to his throat, and demanding disclosure. He thinks the whole world sees it in his face, reads it in his eyes, and almost hears its workings in the very silence of his thoughts.... It must be confessed, it will be confessed!"

Perhaps the murder's widest influence may be on the Salem-based board game makers the Parker Brothers. Parker Brothers began their board game empire from their now-demolished factory on Bridge Street, right here in Salem, the town in which they were born. In 1949, the company bought the rights to the British murder-mystery game of "Cluedo" which they would adapt for an American audience. What better place could they have for a model of the famous "Clue" mansion than the site of an actual American murder mystery which was just steps away from the first store opened by George Parker in 1887?

Whether the Gardner Pingree House inspired the design of the "Boddy Mansion" in the early versions of the game is up for debate, though the interesting inclusion of the character "Mrs. White" (originally "Nurse White" in "Cluedo") and other similarities have earned the Gardner-Pingree the nickname of "The Clue House."

If you are fortunate enough to take a tour of the historic home, do not bother to ask about Captain White, however, as the tours do not mention him, or his famous murder, which may be yet another reason why his spirit still stalks the property he owned, which denies his very name.

Howard Street Cemetery:
The Curse of Giles Corey

Howard Street, Salem

The Howard Street Cemetery lies just outside of the hustle and bustle of downtown Salem. Much quieter and less-visited than the Charter Street Cemetery, it has no less of an engaging history than the older graveyard, and also possesses an infamous connection to the Salem Witch Hysteria.

The cemetery was first put to use in 1801 as a cemetery for "strangers," that is, those who arrived in Salem with no connections to the town and no family. People making their way to Salem in search of fortune was nothing new, especially as the town grew in prosperity following the American Revolutionary War. A number of veterans of the war for American Independence would be interred here at Howard Street.

Elizabeth Clarke Manning, mother of Nathaniel Hawthorne, and her daughters Elizabeth and Maria are buried here as well.

The cemetery also became known for the section dedicated as a site for burials in the African American community. Most prominent among those interred here was businessman, Prince Farmer, who served as a cook on the Salem ship George and went into business for himself after ending his career at sea. Farmer became an oyster dealer and gained great success in this field. Many people in Salem's early African-American community found great opportunity in life at sea, where less concern was placed on a man's skin color than if he were a good hand on deck. As it was for Prince Farmer, oyster-dealing became a path to success for many African-Americans in Salem, including John and Nancy Remond, who were caterers, oyster dealers, restaurateurs, owned an ice cream shop, and still found time to raise seven children. Two of whom, Charles Lenox Remond and Sarah Parker Remond, became internationally reknowned in the fight against slavery. Excepting Sarah, who died in Italy and is buried there, they are interred at Harmony Grove Cemetery.

Across Howard Street was the Howard Street Church, which held meetings of the Female Anti-Slavery Society and lectures by abolitionists. The church also had the uncomfortable feature of having been the place in 1830 where Frank Knapp hid the incriminating weapons the night of the murder of Joseph White (see the Gardner-Pingree chapter). Both Frank and Joe Knapp Jr are buried at the Howard Street Cemetery, along with a number of others who died at the Old Salem Jail, which abuts the cemetery on the north side. The victim of the murder, Captain Joseph White, is buried there as well. Over time, sea captains would be buried at this cemetery; including the heroic Captain William Brown, who managed to evacuate his crew from the ship Brutus which had been caught in a blizzard at sea. Captain Brown's men made it to shore, but thirteen died of exposure while awaiting rescue. Captain Brown was the first to die, having jumped overboard last and clad only in his night-shirt.

The Howard Street Cemetery is known largely as the location of the deadly interrogation of Giles Corey in September of 1692, and the supposed curse created by Corey in his final hours. Giles Corey was a farmer in Salem Fields (modern-day Peabody) who was known for his temper and stubbornness. Corey took no issue with pursuing legal action against his neighbors, suing John Proctor for slander after Proctor accused Corey of setting fire to his home.

Corey's reputation was not a sterling one; many in the town accounted him a murderer for the severe beating he gave to his servant

Jacob Gooddall, resulting in the man's death. Corey struck his servant several dozen times as punishment for a supposed theft, and refused to allow him to see a doctor for three days, after which time Goodall died. Corey did have to stand before this charge, but was not convicted of murder and instead had to pay a fine. Some whispered that Corey may have had some help from the Devil in this escape.

In 1692, he was about eighty years old and wed to his third wife Martha Corey. Martha was accused of witchcraft in March 1692. In her examination, she attempted to defend herself, but was accused of lying immediately and many attested to statements she did not remember making. "What can I do when so many rise up against me?" she cried, to which John Hathorne responded "Why, confess." Giles attempted to persuade her examiners that his wife was afflicted by witches, rather than one of them. However, his claims of her strange behavior and actions only served to provide more evidence against her. She would be sent to the Boston Jail pending her trial, and Giles rode alongside the prison cart most of the road to Boston. He reportedly told her he suspected that he would be joining her soon.

Several weeks later, Corey himself was accused of witchcraft and brought in for examination. Corey insisted on his innocence and would attempt to defend himself, but was seemingly caught in a lie about a statement he had made concerning being frightened in his cow house, and any argument he may have made after was invalidated by the magistrate's suspicion that he was not being truthful. The magistrates decided to move him forward for a trial, but that is where Corey's process deviates from anyone else's in the trials. He had pled his innocence, but refused to accept the authority of the court "before my God and my country." This refusal to speak was called "standing mute" and a proper trial could not commence without this important step.

Sheriff George Corwin and the Court of Oyer and Terminar had been charged by Governor William Phips to proceed according to the laws of England, which was a change from the previous Charter that allowed them to create and follow the Body of Liberties Act of 1641. Torture was allowed in cases on a convicted person as away of getting information about their co-conspirators, however, the Body of Liberties Act read "for bodilie punishments we allow amongst us none that are inhumane, barbarous or cruell." Torture was usually done through neglect or great discomfort, such as what was suffered by William Proctor.

Corwin needed Giles Corey to accept the courts' authority as this defiance would be harmful to the court if future accused followed his example. Corwin was willing to take advantage of that fact that English law gave him an option to get that admission from Corey. Peine forte et dure was used in England in cases where an accused felon stood mute. The phrase translated from French is basically "strong and harsh sentence/punishment." It was achieved sometimes through neglect, but also sometimes in using weights to crush an accused felon into confession. Rarely ever was this form of torture used, as the threat of it was often enough to achieve the desired effect. Colloquially, it may be the origin of the phrases "pressed for information" and "getting the weight off your chest."

In practice, the torture was utterly horrifying and would be used only this one time in American history. The night before the torture began, Ann Putnam Jr had suffered a terrible fit and said that Corey's spectral form had tormented her and told her the Devil had helped him escape hanging for the death of a man; likely Goodall, though the event happened long before Ann was born. The Devil, she said, had hardened Corey's heart.

On September 18th, eighty year old Giles Corey was taken from the Salem Gaol to a pasture beside the gaol that is now the site of the Howard Street Cemetery. He was stripped nude and laid down on a wooden door. Another door was placed over his body. The Sheriff ordered heavy blocks of stone to be placed on top of Corey until he agreed to be tried by the court. This was a public spectacle and though we do not know how many observers were present, several have written of witnessing the event.

It is unknown exactly how long this torture lasted, but one of those witnessing the torture was Robert Calef, an outspoken opponent of the trials who published a damning condemnation of the Court and Cotton Mather, wrote that Corey's "tongue being prest out of his mouth, the sheriff with his cane forced it in again when he was dying." Corey's ribcage broke under the pressure, and death would take him soon after. After his death, a story was spread from an unknown source that Corey had spoken the words "More weight!" shortly before he died. This was not recorded officially in any surviving record, but was a known statement that would be uttered by those suffering piene forte et dure to hasten their inevitable deaths. Corey's death would be largely considered a suicide, as he had submitted to and endured this torture knowing the lethal nature of it. His death is not considered an official execution as he was never convicted.

Martha Corey sat in the Old Salem Gaol just across the road while her husband was tortured to death, and she would be hanged as a witch just three days later. Suffering this fate did largely protect his property, however, since the lack of a conviction meant his property was not forfeit. Martha's property was considered her husband's, so his death without conviction ensured no property would be taken despite her conviction and execution. The Sheriff was only able to claim enough to pay the jail expenses of Giles and Martha Corey, which would be paid by Corey's children.

Sheriff George Corwin would suffer very little legal repercussions for what he had done during the trials. Chief Justice William Stoughton and the Court of Judicature would officially declare Crowin free of any financial responsibility for his actions during the Salem Witch Hysteria. However, shortly after the trials ended, the Sheriff began to suffer from ill health. He experienced a loss of weight and strength and by April of 1696 was in a fragile state. Perhaps as part of his illness, Sheriff Corwin is said to have begun experiencing a recurring event at night. He would awaken unable to move, feeling weighed down by heavy stones across his chest. He was completely immobile except for his eyes, and he began to see the spectral form of Giles Corey at the foot of his bed. One morning, George Corwin was found dead in his bed of a heart attack. He was twenty nine years old.

The phenomenon experienced by Corwin may have more of a medical explanation than a spectral one. The condition "sleep paralysis" produces similar symptoms. The sufferer's brain awakens and is active, but the body is still asleep, evoking the feeling of weight on one's chest preventing movement. Frightened and confused, the victim's brain creates something scary; often a shadowy figure at the foot of their bed. This disorder has shown up in various forms for centuries, leading to the legends of 'incubi' and 'succubi', demons who held down their sleeping victims. Accusations of witchcraft frequently contained reports of victims suffering the symptoms of sleep paralysis, blaming them on the suspected witch. This was most likely the cause in some spectral evidence associated with Bridget Bishop.

There is, however, something that cannot be explained so well with science; a phenomenon known as "the Curse of Giles Corey." Suffering perhaps more than any other victim of the trials of 1692, it is believed Corey's wrath upon those he felt were responsible for his death would echo for hundreds of years. It is believed by some that Corey shouted to the Sheriff as he died, "Sheriff, I curse you and all Salem!" which purportedly echoed across the town. This event is not recorded by any witness, and it is highly unlikely that a man whose ribs were broken and his tongue forced out of his mouth would be able to shout at all, let alone speak a full sentence. However, the belief that Giles Corey's torturous death had cursed the Sheriff was believed by many, including the future High Sheriffs. Many of those sheriffs died of heart conditions and disorders of the blood, enough that it became local legend that the Sheriff's office was cursed by Corey's vengeful spirit.

The ghost of Corey is said to walk the Howard Street Cemetery, enacting his fearful vengeance on the Sheriffs who lived in the Jail-Keepers house at the jail, adjacent to the cemetery. It was High Sheriff Robert Ellis Cahill who first publicly acknowledged the story of the curse, and wondered if it was not the reason for his own heart problems and rare blood disorder, which caused him to step down as Sheriff in 1978, while at the same time the Sheriff who had left office prior to him was dying of a blood condition.

Another part of the Curse of Giles Corey affects the entire town of Salem. The ghostly figure of Corey is not seen at Howard Street Cemetery regularly, but only appears at times when great tragedy is about to be visited on Salem. On June 25, 1914, a number of people living on Howard Street reported the appearance of a man in Colonial clothing walking in the Howard Street Cemetery. The curse of Corey was very likely known at this time, and may have been on the minds of those who saw the apparition. That night, a fire began at the Korn Leather Factory, which was perhaps not-so-coincidentally abutting Proctor's Ledge, the site that would, in 2016, be declared the true site of the executions in the 1692 Witch Hysteria. This fire spread rapidly through the downtown area of Salem, burning a mile of the city in thirteen hours. One thousand, five hundred homes and businesses were lost. Fifty thousand people lost their homes, their jobs, or both, in a single night. Those who stood in awe of the terrifying spectacle of this fire said that it seemed as if the jaws of Hell had swallowed Salem.

Especially since this famous sighting of Corey, the people of Salem have lived in fear of the ghost's return; the vengeful spirit of a man murdered by the law of the town taking out his anger on lawmakers and the descendants of those who allowed it to happen is nothing short of a legendary ghost story. One that, we hope, has seen it's final chapter. There are no more High Sheriffs seated in Salem; the Essex County Sheriff's department has moved to Middleton, and with it, the strange blood-related deaths of the sheriffs have ceased... for now.

The Salem Jail

50 Saint Peter Street, Salem

S tanding just outside the downtown area of Essex Street and towering over the Howard Street Cemetery is the Old Salem Jail. Construction began on the jail in 1811 and it was opened in 1813, remaining active until 1991. This site is considered the longest-operating jail in United States history. The main jail building and the red jail-keepers house, which would be living quarters for the High Sheriff of Essex County, were completed in 1813, as was the attached carriage house. Places of extraordinary suffering and human misery often become centers of paranormal activity and this old jail is no different.

From the time it opened, conditions in the jail were wretched and inhumane. There was a single working toilet in the jail, which inmates were allowed to use once a week. There was no plumbing in any of the cells, so inmates were given a six gallon bucket to use as a toilet in their rooms. Every morning, they would line up to empty their buckets into a sewage funnel located next to the dining hall. The stench would be unbearable throughout the jail and the floor was always covered in filth.

The cells were five foot by eight foot and held two prisoners each. Inmates were allowed one shower per week, perhaps by necessity since the jail had only three showers to accommodate two hundred inmates. Cockroaches skittered across the floor day and night. In the summer, the jail festered with flies and mosquitoes. Violence between inmates and attacks on the guards were a constant problem. Inmates would often dump the contents of their buckets over railings and onto the guards. At least one guard was seriously injured when an entire bucket struck him from several floors up.

The jail was closed in 1991 and prisoners were removed to the new Essex County Jail in Middleton. Some prisoners refused to leave and had to be forced out, hurling their filled metal buckets at the guards. Once the prisoners were gone, a number of the guards chose to vent their frustration by vandalizing the jail, breaking windows, kicking holes in the walls, and smashing televisions and radios. The jail would sit in this empty, filthy state for nearly twenty years. The empty edifice staring out over Bridge Street and the Howard Street Cemetery.

There were not many executions carried out at the jail, but there certainly were a few. The Gallows Hill site would only be used during the Witch Hysteria of 1692, and afterwards the place of hanging would be Execution Hill on Winter Island. Over the course of fifty years, four executions took place at this site, which is now a campground. The highly discussed execution of teenage arsonist Stephen Merrill Clark drew twelve thousand people to the site in 1822, and afterward the place of executions was moved to the Salem Jail. Most notably of these would be the 1830 hangings of Joseph Knapp Jr. and John Francis "Frank" Knapp.

It is the third party to their crime that may be linked to the frightening paranormal activity that has been experienced in this building. Richard Crowninshield, nicknamed Dick, was known as a rough individual from the beginning. He was alleged to have set fire to the schoolhouse due to his dislike of the teacher. You may see the full story of the murder and trials in the Gardner-Pingree section, but it is sufficient to say for the moment that Richard was guilty of the murder but had been arrested on little more than hearsay. Unless more incriminating evidence could be found, he would likely have been released. Richard kept up appearances of his innocence. He would whistle tunes in his jail cell, write poetry and read books. However, his heart must have darkened when he heard that Joseph Knapp Jr, who had hired him to commit the murder, had confessed to everything in order to obtain immunity from prosecution. Joseph provided every detail needed to hang Richard and perhaps his brother George as well, for he had been party to the planning of the murder.

In an act that may have been meant to save his brother's life as well as deny the rabid crowds the opportunity to cheer his certain public execution, Richard Crowninshield stood on a chair and tied a pair of silk handkerchiefs together. He tied one end to the iron bars of his window and the other end around his neck. He stepped off the chair, his hands firming grasping his ankles to make sure his feet did not touch the floor. A guard found him hanging from the window. Attempts were made to resuscitate him, but it was not to be. Crowninshield had left a note for his brother, referencing at length George's innocence in this matter. "Had I taken your advice," he wrote, "I would still enjoy Life, Liberty and a clear conscience." He informed George of the reason for his deadly decision to "deprive them of the pleasure of beholding me publicly executed". Without the conviction of his brother, George Crowninshield had no real connection to the murder and was found not guilty.

Today the old Salem Jail is off-limits to tourists as it is now a luxury apartment building. The high, rusted barbed-wire fences are gone and a pleasant green courtyard spreads out before the former house of correction. However, the jail can be accessed through a restaurant in the back of the building called "Bit Bar." Patrons can view actual former doors, handcuffs and other items from the jail. It is toward the back of Bit Bar that sits the room where the most unusual paranormal activity takes place.

Bit Bar is the latest of several restaurants to occupy this space, and not all have granted access to this back room. Waitstaff at the former restaurant spoke of an unwillingness to go back to that room alone. They would often hear the sound of a man whistling behind them when no one else was there. One member of the staff spoke of feeling cold hands pressed against her back while working there alone. Perhaps most disturbing was the common report of the stench of rotted meat permeating the room. This room is not connected to the kitchen or the garbage room, so no waste smells would be able to waft in. The smell dissipates quickly, and cannot be found again once lost.

This room at Bit Bar is open to any guest, and is now filled with the blinking lights and cheerful sounds of a collection of classic arcade and pinball machines, a far cry from its dark and dismal past.

Saint Peter's Church:
Phillip English

24 Saint Peter Street, Salem

S aint Peter's is a beautiful Episcopal church located on the corner of Brown Street and Saint Peter Street. The instantly noticeable unique feature of the church is the rows of tombstones that are located in front of the church in a fenced-off area. Someone who looks closely to the left hand side of the church will notice an iron gate where, in a narrow alley, several tombstones have been placed in a garden beneath the stairs to the left. The reason for these gravestones' unusual placement goes back several hundred years to the time of the church's founding, and would be the source of a haunting that has frightened nighttime visitors of this area for decades.

The ghostly figure of a black-suited man walking the grounds of the chapel and courtyard behind the church has been seen numerous times over the years. The apparition is best known for his uncommon features; a ghastly smile appears on his face in every instance when he has been sighted. Just who this Smiling Man may be is unknown, though perhaps a look into the bizarre history of this haunted ground may yield some clues as to his identity and the reason for his unsettling appearance.

The land that Saint Peter's was built on was established under the most unusual circumstances. It was once owned by Phillip English, a shipowner from the Jersey island of France. A shrewd businessman, English flourished in Puritan Salem, despite his French heritage and Anglican faith. He married Mary Hollingworth, daughter of Elinor and Richard Hollingworth. Mary's father had been lost at sea, and her marriage to Philip would be a relief to the family.

However, in 1692, both Phillip and Mary would be accused of witchcraft. Susannah Sheldon claimed that Mary English had come to her bearing the Devil's black book for her to set her name in, a yellow bird seated upon her breast. The witches told Susannah she would not be allowed to eat, she said, and was tormented by them the following morning by choking her and knocking the food from her hand and as she tried to eat.

Marshal George Herrick was charged with arresting Mary, which he attempted to do at the family home. The marshal and his men barged into the home and bedroom as the couple slept, and once awakened, Philip fumed as the marshal told them he was there to arrest Mary. Mary carried the situation in a dignified manner, refusing to go with them at such an absurd hour, and stating that she would allow them to take her to jail after rising at her accustomed hour and after breakfast. The marshal agreed and left a man to guard the door. Once Mary had risen at her usual time and only after she had her meal, she went with her guard to jail.

Soon after, Philip was accused of witchcraft as well. William Beal, a man whom he had fought with previously over legal matters, claimed he had seen English's shadowy form creeping around his home, and claimed to suffer nosebleeds whenever discussing their legal issues. Susannah Sheldon said the ghost of a murdered man appeared to her and said that Phillip English had murdered him by drowning him in the sea. Sheldon also claimed that Phillip's spectral form drew a knife on her and demanded that she set her hand to the Devil's book or he would cut her throat and claimed he would kill the governor and many more people.

After dodging the marshal's men for a time, Philip turned himself in so as not to further damage Mary's case. The couple were transported to the Boston jail, from which they miraculously escaped and fled to upstate New York. They waited as the Witch Hysteria ran its course, and soon they returned to Salem. The family would be greeted by a sorrowful sight. High Sheriff George Corwin had seized a great deal of their property. Clothing, furniture, pots, dinnerware and livestock were all gone.

Witchcraft was a felony, and convicted felons could expect to have their property (i.e. goods and cattle) seized upon conviction. However, neither Phillip nor Mary had been convicted of witchcraft. Sheriff Corwin had taken it upon himself to assume that since they fled, they had been guilty. Not one to accept this turn of events without a fight, Philip English sued for restitution. This battle carried on through 1696, and would see the Sheriff, who was at that time growing weak and ill despite his young age of 29, locked up on his own former jail for refusal to pay the debt he owed English.

George Corwin died on April 12, 1696. It is evident that the Sheriff's death did not end English's attempts to reclaim what was taken from him, though the actual means of how he did is still shrouded in uncertainty. Not content to simply fight this battle in court, English may have resorted to more spectacular tactics. There was a custom at the time that a creditor might take possession of the corpse of a dead person until their family paid the debt. Whether English only threatened to do this or whether he actually did remains a macabre mystery. Many years later, English's granddaughter would say that her grandfather had taken Sheriff Corwin's body straight out of the funeral procession and did not return it until the debt had been paid. Rumors would later say the Sheriff was hidden away in the Corwin family basement following this incident, which is discussed further in the Joshua Ward House section.

Philip English's troubles began to pile up once again, this time his enemy was the Salem Church. English was irritated with having to pay taxes for the upkeep of the church that had taken so much from his family in 1692. Mary had died sometime after Corwin's death, and Phillip remarried in 1698 to Sarah Ingersoll. Phillip's refusal to support the church lead into an incident where Phillip publicly denounced the Salem Church as "Satan's Church". He was penalized with a night in jail, after which he grudgingly apologized, but, as events would show, he did not feel truly repentant and likely spent that night fuming with indignation. Perhaps it was then that he came up with the perfect way to take revenge on the Salem Church, while doing a service to the other Anglicans of Salem who were forced to travel all the way to Marblehead for church services.

Phillip English decided would donate part of his property to the Church of England. The Puritans of Salem, who were much like the Pilgrims of Plymouth in trying to create a land free of the influence of the Anglican Church, must have been in quite an uproar. Philip English died in 1736, and was asked on his deathbed if he would be willing to forgive someone who had wronged him, to which he replied that if he were to die that night, he would be forgiving, but if he survived, "I'll be damned if I forgive him."

Phillip English was buried in the graveyard behind Saint Peter's. There is no stone memorializing him, which is believed to be due to English being buried under a different name to protect his resting place from suffering the same indignity as he performed on Sheriff Corwin. Knowing his enemies had been well-served in the end, both the Sheriff and the Salem Church, he may have gone to his eternal rest with a smile. The graveyard he is buried in, however, is hidden in plain sight in modern times.

In 1833, the Episcopal Church of Saint Peter's built a new stone structure on the same site as the 1733 wooden one, even retaining the same pews to this day. A chapel was added to the back of the church, which presented the problem of dealing with the graveyard with over one hundred parishioners buried within. The decision was made to remove the tombstones and build the chapel over the cemetery. The tombstones that sit in front of Saint Peters today have no graves beneath them, the graves are still beneath the chapel and courtyard.

It is on these grounds that the specter of the Smiling Man has been seen. He may appear only in flashes; a portion of head, legs, neck and shoulders usually striding toward Brown Street from the cemetery. He may appear as a column of smoke or steam with no discernable point of origin. The apparition may also appear in the chapel, though that is more rare. One tour guest was horrified to look on a photograph he had taken of the chapel's glass doors only to see the Smiling Man gazing out at him. A Salem resident claimed he had taken a picture into the chapel and seen the image of the smiling ghoul standing before the doors. He fell sick for several days afterward with no explanation for his illness. A year later, he resolved to try his luck again. Once more he took a picture of the chapel doors and was horrified to see that again, the figure was there smiling back at him. He then inexplicably fell ill for several days after. He has not tested his luck a third time.

One of the most important aspects of any sort of paranormal investigation or 'ghost-hunting' is researching the history of the location, and we felt armed with enough information to attempt to learn more about the Smiling Man by trying to contact him. Working with our resident paranormal expert, we attempted to get answers to our questions about his identity using recordings of electronic voice phenomenon (EVP) a tool of paranormal investigators dating back to the Victorian Age, when Americans' fascination with death and ghosts lead them to create the controversial modern science of the paranormal. The first EVP recordings would have been done on Amberol records; wax cylinders that were introduced by Thomas Edison in the 1870s. On our own EVP recording of this graveyard, we asked twenty questions directed at what we assumed was Phillip English. When listening to the playback, we did have some seeming-answers to our questions. When asked what had been taken from him, a voice responded "everything," and when asked if he had hate for anyone, the name "Corwin" came as a reply. The use of EVP is always controversial due to the tendency of the human ear to hear groups of sounds as words and often be influenced by suggestion, but even the most skeptical among us had to admit these answers were chilling.

No member of our team was more frightened that night than the photographer, who took dozens of photos from various points on the sidewalk around the courtyard. As he flipped through his photos at the entrance to the courtyard, he was disturbed to see what appeared to be a face some twenty feet away in one picture. The picture following that showed the same image had moved closer by about five feet. The next picture showed the seeming-glowing apparition closer still. His next photo was blurred out by a strange light. The next photo was the empty courtyard, clear of any image. His heart pounding, he recounted the event to the rest of our team, terrified at the realization that the ghostly figure must have simply walked right through him.

Saint Peter's Church holds one more unusual secret that draws seekers of the paranormal to it. A black door on the Brown Street side of the church is barred from the inside and has scuff marks all over the base of the door. This is due to the popularity of a purported ghostly figure that will often appear standing in the doorway at night. A translucent woman who is shaded grey in appearance reclines in the doorway, her arms resting on either side of the door and her right heel pressed up against the bottom of the door. Fans of ghostly tales will often recline in the doorway themselves, standing in the same position as this Grey Lady, in hopes that she will appear in the photo with them; her spectral form merged with their own.

Danvers State Asylum

1101 Kirkbride Drive, Danvers

High atop Hathorne Hill in Danvers sits the edifice once known as Danvers State Hospital, or the State Lunatic Hospital. Climbing up Maple Street towards the summit is a twisting, turning and confusing path. It is very easy to get lost among the grassy fields, the dark forest of trees, the medical complexes, and large field of corn stalks waving in the wind as you make your way towards the top. This may perhaps be an allegory for the history of the institution that sits at the apex of that hill; good intentions that slowly twisted into a living nightmare for the hundreds of victims who suffered unspeakably within its walls.

Hathorne Hill was chosen to be the location of this much-needed hospital in 1873. This land once belonged to the infamous John Hathorne, remembered as a judge of the Court of Oyer and Terminar during the 1692 Witch Hysteria. The area was chosen due to the remoteness of it; surrounded by peace and quiet overlooking the town of Danvers. The asylum was built according to the Kirkbride Plan; developed by Dr. Thomas Kirkbride, who believed that peaceful surroundings, fresh air and beautiful architecture would greatly benefit the healing process of the mentally ill.

Far too frequently in the past, asylums were little more than prisons where the mentally ill were kept in chains and beaten. Kirkbride and others, like Dorothea Dix, would strive to improve this system. Beautiful gardens, soft music, a general cleanliness and comforting atmosphere were all part of the asylum in its early days. Danvers State should have been a centerpiece to show the Kirkbride plan could effectively treat the mentally ill.

The hospital ran over budget before the doors were ever opened. The enormous gardens would attract visitors from across the state, but were incredibly costly. Danvers State produced its own power and much of its own food and water, but expenses continued to pile up on a budget that had to be approved by the Legislature every year and was rarely consistent, to the point where nurses and aides sometimes feared a paycheck would not come. The asylum accepted more and more patients, quickly leading to overcrowding. Rooms that had been intended to hold two patients under the Kirkbride plan now held five, six or more. Originally built for 450 patients, by 1901 it held over 1,000 patients. An expansion would help alleviate overcrowding for a time, but these new rooms quickly filled as well, and the asylum would be crammed full with 2,400 patients by 1940.

People suffering from serious mental health conditions require constant, thoughtful care to help them to heal. The original mission of the asylum was to cure mental illness, but soon it became more of a prison, though scowling jail-keepers were replaced by gentle-speaking doctors and smiling nurses. In the early days, treatment with medication was still some time off, and more unusual and sometimes horrifying methods would be used instead. Patients might get "water treatment," locked in a tub of cold running water with a plastic seal keeping them in, only their heads kept dry; they might be in this treatment for 24 hours or longer in many cases. Particularly enraged or violent patients would be locked alone in a padded room, left to scream and beat their fists against the walls for hours.

Insulin coma therapy was introduced to the asylum in 1946; a method of controlling patients by injecting them with massive insulin doses daily in order to put them into a comatose state. It was believed that this medically induced coma would cure schizophrenia, but did not produce good long-term results. The most frightening of these techniques would be electro-shock therapy. Patients would be dragged down the halls, screaming and fighting with every step, until they were strapped down to a table. A pair of electrodes would be placed at their temples and electricity, anywhere from 180 to 460 volts, would be applied. The patient's tongue would be restrained by a depressor to prevent injury.

Dr. Walter Freeman, an American neurologist, would arrive at Danvers State at a time when the institution was desperate for a way to control its overcrowded, neglected, and often violent population. Danvers State had a history of experimenting with procedures and medication on patients without their consent, and especially on those patients who had no relatives. Dr. Freeman introduced to the asylum the procedure that he would become famous for; the frontal lobe lobotomy.

Horrifying in its simplicity, the procedure was administered by inserting an ice pick (an actual ice pick) through the orbital socket to sever the nerve tissue in the frontal lobe of the brain. This would result in an instant change in the person, often leaving them devoid of any personality traits of their previous life and reducing the most bombastic personality to a mild and agreeable state, as well as other gruesome complications like the loss of the ability to speak and incontinence. Danvers State earned the nickname "Birthplace of the Lobotomy" and Dr. Freeman would perform several hundred lobotomies at the asylum.

Unexplained deaths seem almost common at the asylum throughout its history. A 70 year old patient was found beaten to death in the hospital. A stick, the likely murder weapon, was found at his side. No arrest was ever made nor any accusation. The murder was simply covered up and forgotten. The same story went for another man in 1952, found beaten to death with a piece of firewood, but no suspect was ever found. In 1970, a young woman died at the hospital which the coroner blamed on the food she had eaten. No conclusions, or penalties, came from the resulting investigation. Many cases of assault on patients would appear in the newspapers, as in a few troubling cases, the people watching over these patients could be seemingly as deranged as those they guarded, or worse.

The methods used by Danvers State Hospital were certainly severe, however in some cases the patients the hospital was presented with were just as terrifying. These halls were once walked by some of the most maniacal criminals that the state had even seen. Early in its history, in 1883, the asylum received Charles Freeman, member of a cult-like religious group, who killed his infant daughter, claiming that he had done so as a sacrifice demanded of him by God. He said in his trial that he had believed she would rise again in three days when he stabbed her as she slept. In 1934, Mitchell Gondak shot and killed a young couple in their home as their baby slept upstairs. He confessed to the crime quickly, stating that he had killed them simply because he wanted to try out his gun. In 1964 millionaire Robert Agassiz Shaw was committed to the asylum following the murder of his 64 year old maid by strangulation. He claimed she was trying to kill him using secret gas jets in his home. Evelyn Roche was convicted of murdering all four of her children by locking them in a car and poisoning them with carbon monoxide gas. She wept as she was sentenced to spend the rest of her life in the asylum. Roche tried to kill herself with her own restraints while in the hospital, and when questioned about the attempt, described the feeling as "not bad at all."

Though it was less than a hundred years old, the asylum had cultivated so much suffering and madness within its walls that it seemed to become permeated by the supernatural. The living screams that filled its corridors would to continue to echo long after the victim had died. One man who worked as an aide at the asylum in his youth said there were many places within the asylums, rooms that were off-limits and never seen open, that sent chills up the spine of any who might carelessly approach them. He did not know what had gone on in these rooms, but every fiber of his being screamed out that he should stay far, far away from it.

Another former aide told of an even stranger experience he had one night at the asylum. Working third shift, he was often the only person on his floor at night, aside from the nurse to whom he made his report. He walked down the darkened halls, past the closed doors of sleeping patients, and saw that one of the rooms had been left open. He approached the room, and saw a patient standing in the very center with his back to the door. "Hey, lights are out, you need to get into bed!" he called out to the patient, who did not acknowledge him and only continued speaking softly to himself. The aide closed and locked the door and continued with his duties. He mentioned the open door to the nurse, and was surprised when she told him no patient was assigned to the room. Frustrated, he marched back to move the patient to the proper room. He unlocked the door and stepped inside. The room was empty. The bed was still untouched. He checked under the bed, but there was nothing there. He checked the windows, but they were still locked and barred as always. He had been the only person with a key on the floor that night, but this person he swore he had seen and heard speaking, now had simply vanished.

Throughout its existence, the horrors of Danvers State and facilities like it all over the country were known to the American people, but often dismissed and rarely ever discussed unless in the event an escaped inmate made the news, or an awful tale of abuse emerged. One person would find immense inspiration in the stories of Danvers State Hospital, the gothic horror writer H.P. Lovecraft. Lovecraft, an imaginatively brilliant and personally controversial author from Providence, Rhode Island (a community established by one of Salem's early ministers, Roger Williams) wrote macabre and outlandish tales that would revolutionize modern dark horror mythology, most famously his "Call of Cthulhu" and stories centered around the Necronomicon.

If Hawthorne and Poe took ghost stories to a new level of art, Lovecraft created entire world mythologies through them. Lovecraft sets many of his stories in the fictional towns of Innsmouth and Arkham. These sleepy New England settings are the backdrop of tales of wizardry and the summoning of ancient gods. The town of Arkham appears based on the seaside community of Salem, shown by his frequent use of old Salem's family names including Derby, Pickman and Crowninshield, as well as locations like the Old Witch House, the Crowninshield-Bentley house and the Peabody/Grimshawe House. In his short story, "The Thing On the Doorstep," Lovecraft adds a new location to his mythology; Arkham Asylum. Lovecraft actually mentions Danvers State Hospital by name in his stories "The Pickman Model" and "Shadow Over Innsmouth". This would lead to another mythology of the old asylum in the DC comic books universe in Batman, as Arkham Asylum appears as a place where Batman's gallery of rogues is often incarcerated, before somehow escaping to run rampant in Gotham again.

Danvers State Hospital would close its doors in 1992. Expense and an overall lack of support for the institution following reports of abuse would lead the Commonwealth of Massachusetts to eliminate the asylum. Patients were sent to one of the other already-overcrowded state hospitals still in operation, mainly in the newly-renovated Tewksbury State Hospital or simply turned out to the streets. The asylum sat vacant for fourteen years, becoming a popular destination for urban explorers and amateur paranormal investigators. Two films feature actual footage of the asylum; Home Before Dark (1958), starring Jean Simmons as woman being released from the asylum, and Session 9 (2001) a thriller filmed in the asylum after its closure.

A developer purchased the property in 2005 and began renovations to turn the decrepit asylum into a residential complex. A fire in 2007 tore through four apartment buildings and destroyed most of the work that had been done up until that point. In 2019, the complex is now opened and largely populated. While the main buildings were demolished and much of the original destroyed in the fire, the facade of the main Kirkbride building was rebuilt and still casts its long shadow over Hathorne Hill.

Our research trip to Danvers State Hospital brought us to a hidden part of the new complex; the Danvers State Cemetery. A gravel path down the hill from the Kirkbridge building slowly winds to the base of the hill through a forest area. We approached the path as the sun set and the insects of the wood began their nightly calls, eerily echoing in the quiet hillside. Further down we found the field of cornstalks that spread across the hill came to an abrupt and unsettling end at this path. The stalks headed toward the cemetery path begin to whither starting about fifty feet away, and are dead and falling into the path at the end of it.

The gravel path leads down to a clearing in the forest, where a large gray stone sits with the words "The Danvers State Hospital Cemetery" inscribed neatly into the rock. Beneath that is the phrase "The Echos They Left Behind." Upon entering the eerily quiet cemetery, we saw small stone pillars with numbers on them, meant to signify the burial sites of patients. In all, there are 770 former patients buried on the grounds at Danvers State, but there are precious few tombstones visible. The Danvers State Memorial Commitee has put in much work to identify the graves of those who are interred, but on our visit, barely any of the markers could be seen through the grass.

At the center of this cemetery is a series of plaques that list the names of all the patients buried on the property. Looking over their names in the silence of this secluded spot calls to mind the chaotic horror with which their daily lives must have been filled, and we hope they have found some peace while resting in this quiet place.

The House of the Seven Gables:
Nathaniel Hawthorne

115 Derby Street, Salem

"Half-way down a by-street of one of our New England towns stands a rusty wooden house, with seven acutely peaked gables, facing towards various points of the compass, and a huge, clustered chimney in the midst." Thus begins Nathaniel Hawthorne's magnum opus, his masterpiece, beloved romance, and ghostly tale, *The House of The Seven Gables*. "The aspect of the venerable mansion has always affected me like a human countenance, bearing the traces not merely of outward storm and sunshine, but expressive also, of the long lapse of mortal life, and accompanying vicissitudes that have passed within."

While Hawthorne's often told tale is certainly set within the actual venerable structure seated on the Salem coast in the heart of the Historic waterfront, the story itself is a finely woven construct based on his personal feelings about the actions taken by the people of his city, and in particular the choices of his ancestor, John Hathorne, during the Witchcraft Hysteria of 1692. Filled with ghosts and curses and star-crossed love, the story has inspired countless authors, and has entwined itself with the very fate of the building that inspired him, even if he never saw it as his cousin described it to him over the course of his many visits.

The House of The Seven Gables is often known by another name, The Turner-Ingersoll mansion. The property was purchased by Captain John Turner, an extremely successful merchant, and had the fine "two by two" structure built in the first period (post medieval) style in 1668. His dealings in the early days would be of the triangle trade, codfish and lumber going to the West Indies for trade in sugar, spices, and rum, which would then be traded for finished goods in England and then back to the New England colonies.

This trade very often included slave-trafficking as well, and though there were not as many African and Native enslaved persons in New England as their would be down South on the much larger farms and plantations, it would be unfair to those affected to pretend that it did not exist. It was through this loathesome trade that people like Tituba and others affected by the Witchcraft Trials came to the colonies. Candy, who confessed that her "mistress," as she referred to her, had made her a witch and was found innocent by a jury in early 1693, Mary Black, enslaved by Nathaniel Putnam, who was held for trial and later acquitted, and Wonn (likely Juan), an African man enslaved by John Ingersoll who claimed to have been afflicted by the spectre of Bridget Bishop, would have been sold to families in the Massachusetts Colony. Homes like the Turner's would have had several enslaved persons in their household, three at least during the time of his son; Titus, Rebeckah and Lewis. Titus was in the home for at least 14 years, having been baptised in 1728.

Indentured servants would also be used during this time to perform the menial tasks of cooking and cleaning, whereas in the less wealthy families of the era, these would be done by the lady of the house and the younger children. Indentured servants were treated nearly the same as those who were more literally enslaved during the colonial era, save that they would not be listed as "property" and their servitude had an expiration as listed upon their contract. Beatings and general ill-treatment were common for both as it did not carry a punishment under English law, and the only thing that would prevent them was the compassion of a particular family for someone they had grown fond of.

The English law allowed this terrible treatment, though the people of the Colonies prior, under the Body of Liberties Act would have followed this ruling; "There shall never be any bond slaverie, villinage or Captivitie amongst us unles it be lawfull Captives taken in just warres, and such strangers as willingly selle themselves or are sold to us. And these shall have all the liberties and Christian usages which the law of god established in Israell concerning such persons doeth morally require. This exempts none from servitude who shall be Judged thereto by Authoritie."

John Turner the First would eventually have several additions added to the home before he passed in 1680, and his son, John Turner the Second would find even more success than his father in trade, and add yet more decoration to the home, outfitting it in the then more popular Georgian style. John Turner II was very well known in the community, even more so after he assisted in the capture of the men of local Privateer turned Pirate, John Quelch, who famously stated to his captors and the assemblage that "they should take care how they brought money into New England lest they be hanged for it" at his execution. His probate inventory was 14 pages long, more than three times the length of the average for the time, and included a fleet of ships, with several wharves in Salem and land in the surrounding communities.

It was his son, John Turner the Third who would sadly lose the home due to his terrible business sense and addiction to gambling, and the home was purchased in 1782 by Captain Samuel Ingersoll. Ingersoll would remove several of the additions to the home to create a more fashionable, square style known as the Federal style of architecture. It was in this form that it would pass to his daughter, Susanna Ingersoll, the keen businesswoman who owned the building during the days when she would receive visits from her second cousin, Nathaniel Hawthorne.

Hawthorne would visit frequently as he was working just down the street at the Custom House, and it was Susanna's eloquent descriptions of the home in its seven gabled glory that led his mind to create the well-loved classic. Susanna never married, and her adopted son Horace, like John Turner III before him, lost the home in 1879 after squandering his inheritance. The house was passed around a bit during the next few years, until the Upton family purchased it in 1883, giving tours of the grand mansion for the first time, and even selling tea cups with "witches" painted on them as a souvenir.

It was in 1908 that its final private owner would buy the Turner-Ingersoll Mansion, and transform it in a miraculous way. Caroline

Emmerton was a remarkable woman, and as a preservationist and devoted fan of Nathaniel Hawthorne, she was able to make a remarkable change to the home, by restoring it to how it had appeared over a hundred and twenty-five years prior, as a seven gabled structure once more. Her fascination with the book led her to craft rooms that seemed as though they were lifted straight from Hawthorne's pages, and with the assistance of architect Joseph Everett Chandler, they created a masterpiece of both preservation and interpretation.

Her most famous addition is the secret staircase which passes up through the center of the home alongside the chimney. While the inspiration comes from both the book and the look of servants' staircases which were commonly hidden in wealthy homes of the time, the staircase seems to have taken on a legend of its own, and has been described as a place for hiding escaping slaves, smugglers, or even Bluebeard-esque murder victims, all of which we assure you are nothing more than myths.

While Hawthorne's ghostly tale is one of grisly murder through ancient curse, taking great liberties with the tale of Sarah Good's affliction of Rev. Nicholas Noyes, Hawthorne himself saw and described his story as a romance, much like Romeo and Juliet. A true romantic at heart, his belief in the power of love seems to always come through, even in his most bitingly satirical and gruesome tales. And though a romance in Hawthorne's eyes, it will still be most famous as a ghost story, influencing the likes of H.P. Lovecraft, who considered it, "New England's greatest contribution to weird literature" and as Hawthorne himself was inspired by Edgar Allen Poe, who deemed him a "privately-admired and publicly-unappreciated man of genius," we see in these three dark romantic authors of the age and their mutual appreciation, the greatest influence on the modern American ghostly tale.

It seems obvious then, for a building so tied to our indebtedness to the present-day interpretations and fascination with the supernatural, to have its own occasions of paranormal activity. There are multitudes of eyewitness encounters of unexplained phenomena, doors opening by themselves, footsteps in empty rooms, or even voices long after the house is clear of visitors for the evening, though you can not expect to hear anything about these on the regular tours.

The actors who perform in the annual events, "Legacy of The Hanging Judge" in Hawthorne's birth home, built in 1750 and originally on Union Street which is now on the property, and "The Spirits of The Gables" in the Turner-Ingersoll mansion have had some of the most unconventional experiences. There have been several accounts of an extra guest amongst the patrons of the performances, dressed in colonial attire, who seems to not be with anyone else, standing slightly further back than the more "earthly" guests. Perhaps the most chilling part of this tale is that no performer has ever seen this person enter or leave the room, they simply seem to appear from amidst the assemblage. Could this be an ancestor or victim of the Hawthorne line, come to bear witness to the apologies of the present day? Or perhaps it is nothing more than someone in colonial costume that jarred the frayed nerves of actors who must wait alone in the darkened chambers of these ancient structures in between performances.

Whatever ephemeral encounters one may have while visiting the Seven Gables property, there is always comfort to be taken in knowing that you are not alone in the experience, and if Hawthorne's own ghosts of his ancestry were conjured into being by his writing of *The House of The Seven Gables*, they are as much a part of the history of the structures as the very beams and nails that form their wooden bones.

The Stephen Daniels House

1 Daniels Street, Salem

Built in 1667 for mariner Stephen Daniels, the "Stephen Daniels House" was once a popular and charming bed and breakfast which sadly closed in 2018. Guests of the inn have many stories of the delightful owner and the comfortable surroundings of this classic colonial home.

While many of the ghostly hauntings within this book are unsettling and scary, it is quite fitting that the haunting of the Daniels house is far more on the cozy side; a ghostly gray cat who walks the rooms of the home. The cat seemed particularly drawn to the Rose Room. For years, guests of the inn have recounted their meetings with the ghostly feline on review sites, claiming that the cat suddenly appeared in their room or sauntered in through the door to their amazed eyes.

Some guests even claim that the cat graciously allowed them to pet him or her. However, there was not only a spectral cat inhabiting the building, but another cat named Sabrina who lived at the home. Perhaps some of these sightings may be attributed to mistakenly believing Sabrina was the ghost cat, but many guests clearly differentiate between seeing the red-and-black coloring (sometimes called 'tortoiseshell') of Sabrina and the deep gray hue of the mysterious ghost cat. Though the inn is no longer operating, it is very likely that the ghost cat still roams its halls, doing whatever it is that spectral cats enjoy.

The Hawthorne Hotel and Salem Common

18 Washington Square W, Salem

The Hawthorne Hotel was built in 1925 to great fanfare and excitement. Over the years, it has been visited by many notable guests including international dignitaries, celebrities and former American Presidents. The hotel appeared in the 1970s television show Bewitched and series star Elizabeth Montogmery and her family stayed at the hotel during filming. The 2015 film Joy starring Jennifer Garner and Robert DeNiro would be filmed there. Many fans of the television series Ghost Hunters will recognize the hotel for investigations performed there by the show.

The Hawthorne is consistently considered among the top ten most haunted hotels in the country. The ghostly sightings within the hotel are often confined to the sixth floor and the third floor. On the sixth floor, a mysterious woman is known to walk the halls, knocking on the doors of the rooms. Guests will open the door and find no one standing outside. The specter will sometimes appear inside the rooms on the sixth floor, but only briefly, as she walks through the chambers; entering from one wall and exiting through the other.

Room 325 is believed to be the hotel's most haunted room. It is a double room, which has two separate bedrooms connected by a bathroom. Guests sleeping in either of the two bedrooms have heard the doorknob turning, the locks shaking and sometimes unlocking themselves. The faucets of the bathroom will turn off and on by themselves, and some guests have reported feeling as if someone is standing in the room with them when in the bathroom. One guest said that when leaving the restroom, she felt the presence of another person standing behind her so powerfully that she felt their breath on the back of her neck. The sound of a child crying will often be heard in the room, even if there are no children on the floor.

Perhaps the most frequent and frightening experience guests will have is to awaken at night and see a woman standing at the foot of their bed. The ghostly figures hand will be reaching down by their feet and they may feel as if icy fingers are playing with their toes. The identity of this ghostly figure is unknown, and there are no known deaths that have occured within the Hawthorne's walls. A ghost may not always specifically be connected to a place of death, and could be connected to an important life event, place of employment, or other strong connection to a site. The Hawthorne today is also home to a yearly paranormal investigator convention each April.

Adjacent to the Hawthorne Hotel is the Salem Common, a place that has been a part of Salem's history from its earliest days. A shared planting field for the first colonists and the Naumkeag tribe, the Common would soon became a place of public punishment. No hangings were done on the Common, but many degrading and painful punishments were handed out here. Offenders might find themselves punished with a stay in the stocks, their head and hands clasped between wooden boards and their hands chained to the post. Onlookers could humiliate and injure sufferers by throwing rocks or clods of manure at them. A whipping post was set up for offenders to receive lashes (or "stripes") with a switch or leather whip. No more than forty lashes could be meted out, for even forty could put a person dangerously close to death, and whipping was not meant to be an execution.

In the fictional Salem of Nathaniel Hawthorne's *The Scarlet Letter*, Hester Prynne most likely would be given her scarlet "A" (to signify adultery) on Salem Common, though in the real Salem of Colonial times she would be branded with her offense by use of a hot iron, never to be free of the mark of sin. Some psychics that visit Salem claim this area has the most powerful negative aura in the city due to its years of misery and suffering.

The history of Salem Common is not entirely negative though, in 1636, this site saw the first muster of the North, South and East Regiments. This event is considered the beginning of the American National Guard, and in 2013 President Barack Obama officially recognized Salem as the birthplace of the National Guard. This history is celebrated every year in April with a recreation of the first muster with the Guard of today and reenactors representing centuries of military life in America.

In the earliest times, a large portion of today's Common was swamp land created by the adjoining of five ponds. In 1801, Elias Hasket Derby had the ponds and swamp filled in to allow for other use of the area. However, the Common today retains one of the supernatural phenomena that are often found within swamps; will-o-the-wisps, also known as "ghost lanterns" or "ghost lights," will appear in some areas of the Common. These ancient lights are frequently seen in the lore of Scotland and Ireland, beckoning unsuspecting passerby to follow them. Those who do, however, will be met with disaster and death. When walking the Common at night, is it wise to keep this in mind, lest a will-o-the-wisp draw you into an unfortunate accident.

The Yin Yu Tang House

161 Essex Street/Exterior Charter Street, Salem

One of the most curious sites in Salem Town is the stunning and delightfully incongruous Yin Yu Tang house. The structure was built over 200 years ago during the Qing Dynasty, in the Huizhou region of Southeast China, in the province of Anhui, village of Huang Cun, by the wealthy and successful merchant, Huang, 28th or 29th generation of his family line. The building was most likely named for the desire to shelter many generations of family.

With sixteen bedrooms and an open air courtyard with koi ponds, it is easily a mansion by the standards of the village, and the only example of Chinese architecture of its type currently in North America. When the last of the family moved away in 1982, after eight generations had lived there, the home was purchased by the Peabody Essex Museum in 1997, and moved, piece by piece to its present site in Salem, and opened to the public in 2003.

The home has a fascinating history as the building stood during the Taiping Rebellion, The Opium Wars, The Boxer Rising, the 1911 Revolution, and of course, two World Wars. To give a parallel to events in the United States, the home was built one year after the founding of the East India Marine Society, which would eventually join with the Essex Institute and be renamed as the Peabody Academy of Science, later the Peabody Museum of Salem, and finally the Peabody Essex Museum.

One would expect a structure of such age and history to have its share of hauntings, but the fascinating thing about this building is that the PEM acknowledges its most famous spirit right on their website. In 1885, the then 32nd patriarch of the Huang family, Huang Yangxian, was travelling to Hankou (now modern Wuhan) by boat, most likely along the Yangtze river, when he was beset by pirates. He was robbed of his belongings, and murdered, his body dumped into the river, and it is never recovered. His wife, Madame Cheng (not to be confused with the famous Pirate Queen 'Madame Cheng' as the name may be similar to the Western 'Jane Doe') was forced to care for her two children by herself, becoming a seamstress and eventually renting out four of the Yin Yu Tang House's rooms to a relative to survive.

Many years later, in 1968, the then new Communist government would send young people to the countryside to deal with overcrowding in the cities, and to have more people producing food and learning about the hardships of working the land. A small military outpost was established in Huang Cun to accommodate this, and dozens of young military students and working women were given a place to stay in Yin Yu Tang. Soon after, the graves of many of the Huang family were unearthed and the belongings of the dead plundered. None of the culprits were ever found.

Now according to Chinese lore, if a person dies and is not given a proper burial, or if their resting places are disturbed, they become a hungry ghost, or Jiangshi. A Jiangshi is a dessicated corpse, hungry for the spirit or "Qi" of the living. Dressed in the traditional garments of the Qing Dynasty, its arms and hands with long nails for trapping its prey outstretched, and because of rigor mortis, forced to hop in order to travel, a Jiangshi would be the most gruesome of sights. Due to this peculiar method of locomotion, the loud knock of a Jiangshi's feet hitting the ground is its distinctive calling card, and many who have travelled along Charter Street at night claim to have heard this ominous sound at the back of the eerily lit Yin Yu Tang.

If you do encounter this fearsome spirit, have no fear! There are several ways of dealing with a Jiangshi. Firstly is the most traditional method of writing a protective charm on rice paper, using chicken's blood, and sticking it to the Jiangshi's face. If you don't happen to have those, you can toss rice at its feet, because similar to the idea of a Western Vampire, supposedly Jiangshi cannot pass by scattered objects without picking up or counting them all. Another option is to ward it off with a piece of wood from a peach tree, which in Chinese lore holds all of the five elements. However if you do not happen to have any of these articles to ward them off, you can simply hold your breath to hide yourself and your Qi from its fearsome hunt.

The Goult-Pickman House

Charter Street, Salem

The Pickman House is perhaps the biggest enigma in the storied annals of Salem. Purportedly built in 1664, it is one of the oldest structures still standing in the city, a beautifully restored building that is one of the finest examples of First Period Architecture that Massachusetts has to offer. It is also, in our humble opinion, the most haunted building in Salem.

There are many tales attributed to the Pickman House. Some say a young girl was abandoned in the attic by her family after she contracted Scarlet Fever, living the rest of her tortured days without the comforting touch of humanity as she eventually passed away in the darkness. Other, wilder stories are told of a candle-maker who tortured either his wife or his daughter to death by dripping hot wax upon her head until she succumbed to burns and suffocation. Of course, no reasoning is given for these dreadful murders, and the story most likely began due to the site's close proximity to Salem's original Wax Museum.

H.P. Lovecraft wrote a story called "Pickman's Model "in which he makes reference to the main character, the gruesome artist Richard Upton Pickman, being descended from one of the victims of the Witchcraft Trials of 1692. In the story, his most horrific painting, "Ghoul Feeding" was in the possession of his father in Salem. Pickman vanishes from his home in 1926, according to Lovecraft's later History of the Necronomicon, and it is stated that one of the copies of the text written in ancient Greek is in the possession of that same Salem family.

The home has a less horrific claim to fame as the temporary residence of Michele Felice Corne, a masterful maritime artist, who despite his name, is credited with convincing the American people that the tomato was not a deadly food, having eaten them regularly in his native land of Elba, an island in the Mediteranean. This house has been closed to the public for over twenty years, and while the exterior is maintained by the PEM, the interior is neglected and quite empty. There are no signs that this was once a very active part of the museum with a display inside that told the story of the Salem Witch Hysteria using mannequins in Puritan costume and pre-recorded narration. There is no more period furniture visible in the home, only modern folding chairs and tables, and everything inside is covered in a thick layer of dust.

The Pickman House at night is home to a frightening apparition that has left many visitors shaking as they walk away. The spectre appears in the form of a young girl in a white shift with long, dark hair covering most of her face. We do not know which of the home's many former inhabitants may have produced this ghostly figure, but one thing that is certain is her interest in the world outside her house. Due to the emptiness of the house, she is quite easily seen when she appears, which will draw gasps of fear from any who chance to look in her windows at the right moment. That she will sometimes turn and stare back at the person watching her will cause terrified screams to pierce the night. She seems particularly drawn to the attic, standing before one of the two attic windows on either side of the home. This lends some spectral credence to the tale that she was a young member of the Pickman (or Pitman) family who died of fever in that same attic, as top-floor rooms in these houses would often become the bedrooms of older children.

The figure is so spine-chilling that when one of our younger guests was asked what the scariest thing she could think of for a Halloween costume was, her answer was the ghost of the Pickman House. The view of the Pickman house from the Witch Trials Memorial provides a clear look up to the second floor via a light that is always left on by the central staircase. While the light is there for the safety of any member of the museum staff that enters the darkened building, it serves the purpose of illuminating the musty stairs that lead up to the attic. She may walk down those steps from her attic, sometimes in full view of crowds of people; the stories of which we have heard many a frightened guest recount.

A darkened, shadowy area next to those stairs seems to be another place from which she likes to peer out at the world. We certainly cannot say if she is sentient or merely an imprint of the energy of a long-past resident, but those who have seen her, swear that she is not just staring blankly, but that she is looking directly at them. One guest of our tours, who stated numerous times early in the evening that she did not believe in ghosts, looked up the staircase of the Pickman house and was immediately stricken with fear at the sight of the spectre standing in the shadows. She claimed the ghost had stared directly at her from the darkness, briefly locking eyes with her before disappearing. Fortunately for this guest, her wife had seen such things before, and was able to assure her that there was no harm in seeing a ghost; frightening as it may be.

This haunting seems to change shape as well, not only appearing as the young girl, but as a tall silhouetted figure with a clearly-defined head, neck, and shoulders, accompanied by what seem to be two blood-red eyes. This form is seen less frequently, but is even more bloodcurdling to those who encounter it. The Pickman House is not a residence, and so there is no earthly harm in looking in its windows, but be aware that when you look in, someone may be looking right back at you.

Harry Houdini:
The Old Salem Police Station

15 Front Street, Salem

T he city of Salem is synonymous with magic and witchcraft. We are a city that prides itself on our spooky Halloween spectacular, "Haunted Happenings," and the entire month of October is a celebration of the eerie and unexplained. In April of 1906, long after the Witchcraft Trials of 1691/2, Salem played host to a man that revolutionized the world of magic in an entirely different way. A man named Erik Weisz, who became known as "Harry Houdini, The Handcuff King," visited our fair city to perform his daring escapes.

Having just finished an extremely successful run in Boston, where he had been for seven weeks, he promised a full 6 shows at the Salem

Theatre, originally built in 1901, and purportedly located at 273 Essex Street. The highlights of his show in Boston had been an escape from a seemingly impenetrable case made by the Seigel Company, a dramatic extrication from double confinement in the "Boston Tombs" (the City Jail), and the frightening, and peculiarly named, "Salem Witches Chair," purportedly a Puritan torture device, but in reality a much more modern invention, having been built and patented in Oakland, Maine by Sanford J. Baker in 1896 for public humiliation of vagrants and hobos. There are two of these chairs currently on display in Maine, one in its home town of Oakland, with one missing from The Samoset Resort in Rockland where it used to be prominently displayed, and one more, which was used in an escape by Houdini's brother, Hardeen, in Bangor, Maine in 1912. Hardeen and Houdini are the only people to have ever escaped from these horrific devices. While the description of Houdini's performances in Salem do not include the "Witches Chair," it is not far-fetched to think that he may have brought it with him and his entourage.

Houdini would preface many of his ticketed engagements with a free show for the local populace, and Salem was no exception. Arrangements were made for Houdini to perform an escape at the police station, 15 Front Street, on April 16th. Houdini was taken with an entourage, including the mayor, Alderman Benson, to the cell room where he completely undressed and was examined by the committee. James Koen and Willard B. Porter of The Salem News described him as a "genial and unpretentious sort of chap, with an eye like an eagle and a marvelous muscular development." He was shown several cells, and asked the committee which one they would like him locked into. They suggested the padded cell, and Houdini responded that it might take too long, and so he was brought instead to a cell at the center of the row. No less than three pairs of handcuffs were placed on his wrists, and two pairs of shackles on his ankles. He was then locked into another cell, and his clothing placed in yet another locked cell.

At 9:12 AM they left Houdini and assembled in the Janitor's office, which was on the first floor and overlooked Front Street. At 9:25 they heard a voice calling to them from outside the window, and lo and behold, it was Houdini, a mere 13 minutes after they had left him. Houdini was fully dressed, and he was not alone, handcuffed to him was Robert McCoy, a prisoner in one of the other cells. Houdini had, in those 13 minutes, removed three sets of handcuffs, 2 leg shackles, unlocked his cell, unlocked the cell that contained his clothing, dressed himself, unlocked McCoy's cell, left through two locked back doors, and run around the alley by the building to appear triumphantly on Front Street. "Marvelous" said The Salem News, "is the only word to describe the feat." Needless to say, Houdini had no trouble selling tickets to his shows.

Houdini's performances themselves were fairly typical of his tour at the time. He was one of several "Handcuff King" performers, yet he was beginning to become the frontrunner of the pack. As was his wont, he would issue challenges to locals and business owners to attempt to contain him. Almy, Bigelow & Washburn put out a large print ad in The Salem News that "Houdini has accepted a challenge from our shippers and packers to nail and rope him up in a packing case at Salem Theatre this evening" on April 17th. He was locked in a stout barrel with straps and padlocks, and this all placed inside the facsimile of a German prison cell. Mere moments later, he was out, and his assistant who had been in front of the crowd while Houdini had been entering the trap was discovered inside the very barrel Houdini had just left, all locks and straps intact.

The Handcuff King performed liberations from multiple devices of entanglement, however, the highlight of the show from all accounts was a "surprise" disentanglement from a straight jacket, provided by local officers Duffee and Cassidy. Houdini threw himself upon the floor, dislocated his shoulders so that his hands were above his head, and having only a moment of difficulty with a leather strap that had been placed around his neck, was extricated in only a minute and 29 seconds, purportedly less than a third of the amount of time it had taken for him to be bound into it.

Houdini himself was not the sole attraction of this performance, though he was certainly the star. A troupe of Japanese jugglers, the dancing Althea sisters, Miss Anna's singing and impersonations all went over quite well with the audience. The Zancigs, an unassuming pair, performed feats of telepathy, reading names on bank bills, time on watches, and dates on coins from a partner in the audience. A delightful note from the news article makes mention that Miss Lillian Althea sang during this act but, "it was not at all necessary." From reports in the newspaper, the crowds were "large and fashionable" and it seems that each of these shows was sold out.

A peculiar piece came to our attention during the research into Houdini's performances. A small article makes mention of Houdini's visit to the "Peabody Academy of Sciences" a precursor to the now world famous "Peabody Essex Museum." Whilst looking over a selection of handcuffs donated to the museum from the collection of C. Erskine and purportedly from the Wilkes Expedition (though the newspaper mistakenly refers to it as the "Walker" Expedition), he discovered that a pair supposedly used on the USS Vincennes during that expedition were in fact manufactured in the 1880s, not the 1838-1842 listed on the display. Houdini noted that the patent date on this particular piece had been eaten off with acid. He was so assured of his handcuff knowledge, that he volunteered a donation of $1000 to any charity of the Mayor's choice if he could be proven incorrect in his statement. Mr. John Robinson, the curator of the museum discovered the piece in question without incident, and found that while they were labelled "Sailor's Handcuffs," there was nothing about them that said that they were specifically from the expedition, merely that they were another example of pieces used by sailors on shipboard, a very clever way of saying that while Houdini was not incorrect in his assessment of the piece, the museum did not have them mislabelled either. After some communication with the PEM, we have discovered that those same handcuffs are still in the possession of the museum.

Houdini passed away on Halloween, October 31st, of 1926, after what was possibly an intended attempt on his life. Houdini would challenge people to punch him in the stomach after flexing his impressive abdominal muscles. On October 22nd, a student named J. Gordon Whitehead questioned Houdini about this tradition, and without giving the magician time to prepare, hit him several times while he reclined on a sofa, which according to onlookers appeared to pain Houdini greatly. It was only a few days later that Houdini passed, the official cause of death being a ruptured appendix. During his life he had made many enemies as a disprover of fake "Spiritualists" and Mediums who he detested for their preying upon the bereaved, and many believe that Houdini's encounter with Whitehead was an assassination in their name. For ten years following Houdini's death, his wife Bess held a seance to attempt to contact her beloved husband, as they had both held great hope for an existence "on the other side," but after those ten years with no luck, she declared that "ten years was a long enough to wait for any man" and the secret passphrase that they alone had shared was given to his brother, Hardeen, and has since been passed on to family friends and confidants.

Salem played host to a Houdini seance on October 30th, 1990 in the grand ballroom of the Hawthorne Hotel. Though they were unsuccessful in contacting Houdini, the event was the impetus for the beginning of the Hawthorne Halloween Ball, which began the following year and has become the preeminent Costume Ball in the country. Though we talk about many specters appearing in Salem over the years, we have yet to hear a story of someone seeing the easily recognizable figure of Harry Houdini. Though we are less than a decade away from the hundredth anniversary of his death at the time of this writing, perhaps we will be able to host the official seance here one more time, and have the chance for the repeat performance Salem was never gifted with during his mortal lifespan.

The Old Town Hall:
Derby Mansion

32 Derby Square, Salem

The Old Salem Town Hall, built in 1816, is the oldest standing local government structure in Salem. Many visitors to Salem make the Town Hall a priority on the list of sites they want to visit, especially since it was featured in the popular Halloween movie Hocus Pocus. The town hall was the site of the spectacular dance scene where Bette Midler performed "I Put A Spell On You." Today, the Old Town Hall still sees quite a bit of dancing; the second floor serves as a function hall, which has played host to events like the annual Witches' Ball, the Vampire Masquerade, and the Christmastime Fezziwig's Ball, a

Victorian holiday party inspired by Charles Dickens' A Christmas Carol. Local wine and gift shop Pamplemousse has sponsored two annual events here; the 'Spring Fling Bacchanalia' and the Harvest Festival. This historic building is often the site of proms, weddings (including our own wedding reception), theatre performances, art exhibits and concerts. The bottom floor is a museum featuring artifacts from the history of the city.

The Old Town Hall may host many exciting events, but it does have a more frightening side to it, that of a haunting that has been affecting guests and employees ever since the building first opened. Employees today will often talk about the ghostly figure of a woman in a black dress who walks the Town Hall at night. They will hear shouting, or heavy footsteps coming from the second floor, sometimes going up and down the stairs. Exhibits have been found to be moved around at night, knocked over, and sometimes broken on the floor. Some of them have reported the sensation of a hand on the back of their neck that pushes them when walking down the stairs. One man said he was pushed down the steps in front of the building, nearly colliding with the brick walkway outside, but when he spun around to confront who had done it, he saw no one there.

We cannot be certain of the identity of this Lady in Black, but the history of the Town Hall may provide some clues. The area is known as Derby Square; before there was a town hall here, there was a mansion belonging to Elias Hasket Derby, the first recorded millionaire in United States history. Derby's rise to prominence began during the days of the Revolutionary War and surged after the war ended when he established trade routes to India and China. Salem quickly became America's richest city. Derby owned a fine mansion on what is now Derby Street already, the Richard Derby House, and was in the middle of building a grander estate, known as the Hawkes House, when his fortunes fully blossomed. Derby had a great estate built where the Town Hall is now, which was incredibly opulent and grandiose, but he himself did not live in it long, passing away in 1799.

One who seemed very much to enjoy the grand nature of the mansion was Derby's eldest daughter, Elizabeth Derby. Reverend William Bentley, whose diaries tell us many of the intimate details of the lives of the people of Salem in the 1800s, wrote in 1806 of his less-than-glowing opinion of Elizabeth. He believed her to take after her mother, Elizabeth Crowninshield Derby, in being "well known for vanity," and chided the daughter for being stubborn and short-tempered like her father. Vengeful, quarrelsome and "savage" as Bentley put it, Elizabeth would often allow her anger to get the better of her, and is said to have smashed objects in the home, stormed through the halls and up and down the stairs in a rage. If an unfortunate servant happened to be on the stairway at the same time, she was known to force them down the stairs before her, pushing them with no care for their safety.

Her unhappy marriage to Captain Nathaniel West was a source of public scandal. West worked for her father, and the two eloped in 1783. Her father had not been happy with the match as Captain West was far below her station in society, but Elias eventually seems to have somewhat warmed up to West. After Elias Hasket Derby died, Elizabeth had hoped to inherit the family mansion, but this went to her brother Elias Jr. instead. The couple instead inherited the family's farm in Danvers, but it was not long before the shine wore off. Elizabeth wanted to divorce her husband, but the law of the time said that if she did so, the vast fortune she brought into the marriage would go to her husband, as a woman's property belonged to her husband once married. She would only be entitled to a third of what they had together, though her own inheritance from her father greatly dwarfed Nathaniel's earnings. Elizabeth bided her time.

In 1806, the law changed to allow an exception in cases of adultery. A woman who could prove her husband had been unfaithful could have all that was rightfully hers. When this change occurred, Elizabeth filed for divorce from Nathaniel. This was the talk of the town and Elizabeth planned to prove her husband's infidelity in a spectacular and mortifying fashion. During the divorce proceedings on November 11th, Elizabeth brought forward at least thirteen prostitutes who would vouch that they "knew" her husband quite well, one even claimed he was the father of her son. As Bentley reported in his diary, he had seen "all the sweepings of the brothels of Boston and all the vile wretches of Salem, Marblehead, Cape Ann etc." that day, and he lamented for the humiliated Captain West, saying "no person can be safe in his reputation after such proceedings." Public sentiment seemed to go the same way, for the Derby's friendship with the judges in this proceeding was quite clear, and many were horrified at the lengths to which Elizabeth had gone through to ensure her now ex-husband would be ruined in reputation forever. Bentley decried "the shameful pains to which Mrs. West had waded in every filth."

In the end, however, Elizabeth got exactly what she wanted, and Nathaniel could not count a penny of her fortune as his own. As many others had learned before him, it was not wise to anger a Derby. Elizabeth returned back to the farm in Danvers, which was now entirely her own. Perhaps she yearned to retire to that glorious mansion she loved so well, but it was not to be. Elias Jr. found that the mansion was far too expensive to keep up and finding a buyer was next to impossible in those days at the beginning of Salem's decline in fortune. A decision was made to give over the land on which the mansion was built to the town of Salem with the provision that commercial use had to be made of the property. The mansion was torn down, and soon after, the Town Hall was raised in its place.

Elizabeth Derby died in 1814, having spent years alone and unwelcome in the households of the wealthy, respectable families of Salem. It was not long after the Town Hall was built that stories of the Lady in Black began to circulate. It may be that Elizabeth felt that if she could not stay in the mansion when she was alive, in death it would be hers eternally.

In 1834, the Town Hall saw a group of men chained before it whose reputations as rogues, rascals, thieves and killers would be remembered throughout Massachusetts for their infamy. The crew of the ship Panda was lead by the notorious Captain Pedro Gilbert, known to his men as "Don" Pedro. Gilbert was a Spanish pirate with reportedly dashing good looks and a flashy, fashionable style, but possessing a heart of the coldest stone.

The story of Salem's connection with this infamous man begins in late 1832 with the Salem ship, the Mexican, which had left port some months before, under the command of Captain John Butman. The ship carried twenty thousand dollars in silver, meant to be used for trade with Argentina, but the Panda intercepted the Mexican on open water, and Gilbert demanded to be let on board to "inspect" the cargo. The sailors resisted, and the pirates boarded the ship. The crew of the Mexican were locked in the hold, nursing injuries, though none had been killed in the fighting. The pirates emptied the ship of silver. As they prepared to leave the ship, one of Don Pedro's crew asked what to do about the captives. The captain heartlessly replied, "dead cats don't mew." This phrase may well be the origin of the famed fictional pirate motto, "Dead men tell no tales."

Though it is unclear if he spoke this in his native Catalan or Portuguese, a member of the Salem crew understood what the pirate had said and translated for Captain Brown; the pirates meant to kill them all! Gilbert's men lit a fire on the Mexican and then returned to the Panda, content to let her burn and the helpless crew with her. However, Captain Butman was prepared. The sailors pulled a barrel of water to the locked door of the hold and drenched it with water to prevent it from catching fire. Once they were sure the pirates were gone, they broke down the door and escaped on to the deck and put out enough of the fire to keep themselves safe. They left wood burning in a controlled fire so that it would appear to the pirates that the ship was still aflame. They returned home and alerted the authorities of the attack by the dreaded pirates. It took several years, but the Panda was captured in 1834 after a fight with the British navy.

The pirates who survived the fight were brought back to the port of Salem on the British man-o-war Savage and delivered before the Old Town Hall in shackles to the cheers and jeers of hundreds of spectators. The pirates would be transferred to Boston to await trial for their vicious deeds. Most of the crew was convicted and sentenced to be hanged. One pirate "turned state's evidence" and confirmed the guilt of the other pirates in exchange for immunity. A fifteen year old boy named Costa was not convicted, nor was an African servant to the pirates named Antonio, who was assumed to be enslaved by the pirates and therefore could not be considered a willing participant. Interestingly enough, one of the two judges presiding over this case was Supreme Court Justice Joseph Story, a well-known opponent of slavery who would also preside over the famous Amistad case.

One crew member, Bernardo de Soto, was found guilty, but the jury asked for special consideration in his sentencing, as he was known to have rescued forty people from a burning ship some time before and was considered a hero in Havana. In the time following the conviction, de Soto's wife Petrona arrived from Spain to New York City and begged for mercy for her husband from American President Andrew Jackson, who was moved by her words and her husband's heroism and granted clemency.

Such would not be the fate of Captain Pedro Gilbert. He stood as the jury foreman read the verdict of Guilty, and gave the man a gentlemanly bow of the head as he finished. Several months later, the sentence of death was to be carried out on the hapless crew. One pirate managed to cut his own throat in an attempt to avoid a public hanging, but the dead man was placed in a chair on the scaffold with the other pirates, still to hang for his crimes. Captain Gilbert declared the innocence of his crew for all to hear, "Boys, we are going to die," he said, "but let us be firm for we are innocent." The pirates were said to have met their fates bravely and without any outward displays of fear. A fitting end for the lives of these dastardly but proud pirates, who would be the very last crew hanged for piracy in the United States.

The Salem Harbor:
Noah's Dove

160 Derby Street, Salem

Ocean waves gently roll over sand strewn with broken pieces of ancient artifacts from Salem's golden age of sail, while gulls cry overhead and the restaurants that bedeck Pickering Wharf flick their lights off one by one. The harsh clang of metal ties and ropes that make up the rigging of the ships Friendship and Fame echo across the harbor, and the red glow of the ever watchful eye of the Derby Wharf Light Station casts an eerie pall on the moon drenched dark waters of the harbor. It is in this place, in the twilight shadows of the sea captains' mansions and brick edifice of the Custom House that saw trade from the furthest ports of the rich East, that one can truly step back in time, and see Salem as she was in her fullest glory.

As much as Salem has its name forever tied to the infamy of

the Witchcraft Hysteria of 1692, it was this perfect natural harbor that put Salem quite literally on the map. Many maps drawn up during this time from other countries would have "Salem" written upon the entirety of the American Colonies, so much trade came from this one bustling port, that people assumed that it must be the name of the entire country. Protected from the North by Beverly, and from the South and East by the outcropping of Marblehead, until such time as the ships became too large for the shallow harbor, Salem was by far the busiest shipping port in the Colonies.

The earliest settlers of the area now known as Salem were the Naumkeag, a tribe of natives that covered much of current Essex county. The name of the tribe supposedly comes from the words for "fishing place" and is often used as the early name of the land now known as Salem (Old Naumkeag), the Naumkeag people, however, only ever used the term to describe themselves, and the translation may be more along the lines of "People of the Good Fishing Place."

By the time of the founding of Salem in 1626 by Roger Conant, the Naumkeag people had already been nearly wiped out by illness and war with the Tarrantine people of Northern New England which was exacerbated by a plague beginning in 1617. Their Sachem, leader of the Pawtucket Confederation, Nanapeshmet, had been killed by the Tarrantine in 1619, and his wife, known only as Squaw Sachem meaning "the Great Mother," had taken over the governing of the confederacy after his death. Her son, Wenepoykin, was Sachem when the Winthrop fleet arrived in 1629 to officially colonize the area, though he was still quite young, and governed with the assistance of the few remaining tribe elders. A new plague brought by the English, smallpox, would tragically decimate almost all of the Naumkeag by 1633.

The Naumkeag themselves only ever had peaceful dealings with the Salem colonists who came to share their land, and the reverse was true, with much trade between their settlements, but for the most part the early Salem people were terrified of the natives. King Philip's war, with its many raids by the French and their Native allies in Maine, and attacks on the Plymouth colony to the South, would have been very much on the minds of the Salem settlers.

Salem's harbor remained the most frequented in Colonial America until such time as the ships began to be built too large to be handled by the fairly small and shallow port. It was nearly overnight that the shift occurred, and Salem suffered many years of difficulty in finding its niche including the setbacks of the Great Salem Fire in 1914 and later the

Depression.

Slowly the city would reclaim its place as a destination through the growth and popularity of the Peabody Essex Museum, the success of the Parker Brothers and their board game empire, and the revitalization of interest in the Salem Witchcraft Trials thanks to the wildly inaccurate but poignant depiction of them in Arthur Miller's The Crucible. In 1982 the first Haunted Happenings Festival was held, and the city whose name had been made with its flourishing sea trade became known from that point on for its deep ties to the supernatural.

The two are not mutually exclusive however, as one of Salem's most ancient ghostly tales is of the ship Noah's Dove, with her otherworldly passengers and disastrous fate. Known as the Spectre Ship of Salem, the story goes that one fateful day a young man and his bride appeared as if from nowhere in the town, and booked passage on the ship bound for Old England. The couple had an air of unearthly beauty, and those that saw them swore that they must be demons, so perfect were their countenances. The couple stayed in seclusion until such time as the ship was ready to set sail.

On the fateful day that the ship was to cast off, the town had an air of great sorrow and dread, a raven, black as night alighted upon the hand of the great clock and pushed it forward ten minutes. An ill portent indeed, and the family and friends of those others who had booked passage urged them to stay behind, but they would not be swayed. As the ship took sail and swiftly vanished into the distance, the preternatural bride was said to be weeping. As the denizens of Salem Town returned to their homes in dismay, a tremendous storm swept in from the sea. Though it was mid-summer, the town was pelted with hail, and the skies raged with lightning and reverberated with the crash of thunder. For three days the storm raged, and upon the fourth the skies cleared, and the townsfolk went to the shore in hopes of discovering survivors of the wreck of Noah's Dove, which must surely have perished in the gale. Not a scrap of wood was to be found however, though they searched the entire day.

As night fell, a cry arose from a particularly astute observer, as upon the horizon, they spied the familiar masts and rigging of the ill-fated ship. The delight of the onlookers was short lived however, as a sensation of horror washed over them. The ship was indeed Noah's Dove, but she was lit with an eerie glow that shone keenly in the blanketing twilight. As she came closer, Reverend Zebedee Stibbin stood upon a rock at the shore and begged the assembled personages to pray with him, for it must indeed be the work of the spirits that brought the visage to them. Not in any way dissuaded from her course by the prayers, the ship made its way almost to the shore, and the friends and loved ones on board could be seen as clearly as day, yet no sound was heard. At the prow of the ship, clasped arm in arm, were the mysterious couple whose coming had foretold the dreadful fate of Noah's Dove. With a bolt of lightning appearing from the starlit sky, the ghost ship sank into the harbor, never to be seen again.

Many seem to think that this venerable tale of maritime phantasm was transcribed by Cotton Mather from a letter from his friend, the Reverend John Pierpont, describing an event that took place in 1647. The truth of the matter is that while there is a letter from Pierpont to Mather in his book Magnalia Christi Americana explaining a similar tale of a ghostly ship that travelled upon the air, the details and location appear to be a later adaptation, as Pierpont's story takes place in New Haven. This particular version first appeared in Blackwood's Magazine in early 1830, and was then rewritten as a poem by noted Quaker Abolitionist and Poet Justin Greenleaf Whittier. The original is written as though taken from Cotton Mather's works, but with additional details that Mather may not have known, and was written under the pseudonym, Nantucket.

It has been ascribed to many potential authors, including our own Nathaniel Hawthorne, or far more likely, John Neal of Portland, Maine, who often wrote for Blackwood's. To this day, as twilight falls and the mists roll in, some will say that they too have seen a spectral ship in the darkened waters of Salem harbor.

Whether a complete fabrication, a clever reimagining, or the actual truth behind Pierpont's tale, Noah's Dove is a matter of your own belief and investigation. This is also a fair statement as it applies to all the tales contained herein. Our history is as thoroughly researched as is possible at the time of writing, though of course new facts are always being brought to light as more and more generations put their efforts into research.

Our ghostly accounts however, are those of personal experiences and local legend, and the choice to believe them or not is yours. We can only hope, in the telling, that you have been as convinced as we are that there are indeed wonders in the Invisible World, and Salem is one of the finest places to seek them.

Acknowledgements

This book would not be possible without the stories of so many locals and visitors who have joined us on our tours over the years. They have brought to life in front of our very eyes so many of the tales that we thought only legend. We want to thank each and every person who has gone on a Black Cat Tour from the bottom of our hearts.

We would also like to thank our guides and security over these past years for their contributions as well. Whether they still work with us, or have gone on to other things, they are part of our tour family, and several of their stories are told in this book. Thank you Kristin Harris, Amy Sheridan, Johnbarry Green, Adrianna Neefus, David Stickney, Jeff Horton, Olivia Giroux-Galpin, Kevin Harrington, Vincent Morreale, C.T. Hannon, and Douglas Fisher. You guys rock.

An extra special thank you goes to Elizabeth Peterson of The Witch House, and all our co-workers there who made it such a special place to work and develop our first real interest in the stories of The Witchcraft Hysteria.

Likewise, we are grateful to Anne Lucas for bringing us into the House of The Seven Gables family, and our co-workers there over the years for their dedication to historical preservation and interpretation, and most of all, their sense of humor.

Thank you to Professor Dane Morrison of Salem State University, who instilled such a passion for the Maritime History of Salem, which is honestly our favorite subject to discuss.

Thank you to Magdelen "Cricket" Higgins, whose drawn art and carvings have graced our advertisements and signage since the beginning and always exceeds our expectations. You are amazing.

Thank you to Jodi Purdy for her help travelling to some of these out of the way locations, and for her insight and friendship.

Thank you to all our Pastimes friends for creating such vivid characters of some of the people, especially pirates, which we discuss. When we write about them, we can only think of you.

So much thanks goes to everyone at Pamplemousse for all they do to help Black Cat! We are beyond grateful.

Thank you to the members of the many groups on Facebook that have been invaluable resources in fact-checking, detail gathering, and sensitivity. There are too many of you to name, but special thanks goes to the members of the "Salem History Exchange," you have been amazing at helping us find the right paths, and to the many BIPOC for their work to help inform us in finding ways to handle certain subjects with care and respect.

Thank you to everyone who works at the Salem Library for putting up with us running in just before closing far too often. We couldn't have done this without you!

And finally, an absolutely massive thank you goes to Marilynne K. Roach, whose tireless efforts in cataloging the events of the Witchcraft Hysteria in her Day-By-Day account made looking up the original documents a thousand times easier. This book would not have nearly as accurate a history without her undertaking.

Works Cited and Suggested Reading List

Anderson, Katherine & Duffy, Robert. Images of America, Danvers State Hospital Arcadia Publishing, Charleston, SC. 2018

"The Body of Liberties Act." https://history.hanover.edu/texts/masslib.html

Bentley, William D.D. The Diary of William Bentley Vol. 3 1803-1810 Essex Institute. 1962

Booth, Robert. Death of an Empire Saint Martin's Press, New York, NY. 2011

Bradley, Howard. Daniel Webster and the Salem Murder Artcraft Press, Columbia, MO. 1956

Cahill, Robert Ellis. The Wayward Sheriffs of Witch County Old Pine Tree Publishing House, Kissimmee FL. 2004

Calef, Robert. More Wonders of the Invisible World Boston. 1700

Cordingly, David. Under the Black Flag, The Romance and the Reality of Life Among the Pirates. Random House, New York, NY. 1996

Fox, E.T. Pirates in Their Own Words Fox Historical, 2014

Hawthorne, Nathaniel. Twice-Told Tales American Stationers Co. Boston, MA. 1837

Hawthorne, Nathaniel. The House of the Seven Gables Ticknor and Fields, Boston, MA. 1851

Klinger, Leslie S. The New Annotated H.P. Lovecraft Liveright Publishing Corp, New York, NY. 2014

Mather, Cotton. Magnalia Christi Americana Boston, MA. 1702

Mather, Cotton. The Wonders of the Invisible World Boston, MA. 1693

McAllister, Jim. A Brief History of Historic Salem Inc. Salem, Massachusetts Historic Salem Inc, 1994

Nantucket. "The Spectre Ship of Salem" Blackwood's Magazine. March, 1830

Norton, Mary Beth. In the Devil's Snare, the Salem Witchcraft Crisis of 1692 Vintage Books, NY. 2003

Philbrick, Nathaniel. Mayflower The Penguin Group, NY . 2006

Poe, Edgar Allen. The Complete Tales and Poems of Edgar Allen Poe Barnes and Noble. 2015

 Roach, Marilynne K. The Salem Witch Trials: A Day-By-Day Chronicle of a Community Under Siege Taylor Trade Publishing, Lanham, MD. 2004

Roach, Marilynne K. Six Women of Salem; the Untold Story of the Accused and Their Accusers MJF Books, NY. 2013

"The Salem Witchcraft Papers." http://salem.lib.virginia.edu

Snow, Edward Rowe. Pirates and Buccaneers of the Atlantic Coast Yankee Publishing Co. Boston 1944

Szot, Angelina & Stilwell, Barbara. Danvers State: Memoirs of a Nurse in the Asylum, AuthorHouse, Bloomington, IN. 2004

Ward, Gerald W.R. The Gardner-Pingree House Essex Institute, Salem, MA. 1976

Meet the Authors

Lara Fury was born in Cummington, Massachusetts and has lived in Salem for twenty years. She has spent decades working in house museums and giving historical tours. She is a sword fighting instructor, stunt performer, actress, model, and professional pirate. She will soon be pursuing a Masters in Maritime History. She is beyond grateful to Dan for his support, and being the other half of her brain during this writing process and beyond.

Daniel Fury was born in Braintree, Massachusetts and has lived in Salem for thirteen years. He is a playwright and actor. He has been a tour guide in Salem for ten years and loves sharing its stories with our guests. He is grateful to work with Lara on this book, and for her passion and respect for the people whose stories we tell.

Interested in Learning More?

When visiting Salem, please take one of our tours!

www.BlackCatSalem.com

We hope to see you here!

Printed in Great Britain
by Amazon